北京

Beijing

中国民族摄影艺术出版社

CONTENTS

目录
Contents

文物古迹
Places of Historical Interest

悠久的历史为北京留下了无数具有极高审美价值和文化价值的胜迹。北京现有文物3550处，这些珍贵的历史文物就像颗颗璀璨的珍珠，在北京的大地上熠熠生辉。

A long history has left numerous famous historical sites which possess great aesthetic and cultural values. Currently it boasts 3,550 monuments and cultural relics. These relics of historic value are like pearls shining on the land of Beijing.

长城
Great Wall

明十三陵
Ming Tombs

周口店遗址
Zhoukoudian

雍和宫
Yonghegong

京城文化
Beijing's Culture

北京既有深远的风俗积淀，又有融进了不同时代的特色与各国、各民族的精华，所以形成了独特的"京味儿"文化。"京味儿"文化，是以中国北方生活为基础，京城文化为内涵，汉族习惯为主体，又吸纳与融合其他文化而形成的。

Beijing has a strong flavored custom that integrates the essence of all eras and all nations. Based on the lifestyle of North China, Beijing's culture emerge with its own cultural characteristics, mostly the Han culture, while combining those of other places in China as well as foreign cultures.

胡同
Hutong

四合院
Siheyuan

京剧
Peking Opera

传统商业街
Traditional Streets

都市景观
Modern Attractions

北京是著名的历史文化名城，拥有数不胜数的名胜古迹；同时，北京又是一座非常现代化的都市。

Beijing is well known as an ancient city with numerous places of historical interests. However, today's new Beijing is more charming and attractive with its growing prosperity.

目录

前言

　　北京，驰名世界的历史文化名城，是中华人民共和国的首都，也是全国政治、经济、文化、交通和对外交流的中心。全市面积约1.68万平方千米，现有人口1300万，为世界上的特大型城市。北京地处温带半湿润地区，属大陆性季风气候。冬天干寒，夏天暖湿，季节分明，一年四季皆宜旅游，春暖花开和秋高气爽之际，更是旅游的黄金季节。

　　北京，位于中国华北大平原的北端，大自然赐予了北京优越的地理环境和宜人的温带气候。早在50万年前，就有人类的祖先在这里点燃了远古文明的星星之火；在3000多年以前，北京就已经形成了世界上最早的城市之一；在800多年前，北京就拥有了国都的地位。

　　公元10世纪上半叶，中国东北的少数民族契丹建立辽朝，并举兵南下，将北京作为辽的陪都，改称南京，又叫燕京。一个多世纪以后，另一个少数民族女真人建立的金朝将辽灭亡，并于1153年迁都燕京，改名中都。1214年，金朝因受到新兴的蒙古族军队的进攻，迁都汴京（今河南开封），第二年蒙古铁骑入占中都。1267年，蒙古族首领忽必烈下令在中都城的东北郊筑建新城——大都。四年后，忽必烈在兴建中的都城内登上皇帝宝座，建立元朝。1368年，朱元璋在南京建立了明朝。但

分封于北京的燕王朱棣在朱元璋死后即发动战争，并于1402年夺取皇位。第二年，朱棣决定迁都，并开始大规模重建北京。营建工程完成后，明朝于1421年正式迁都北京。1644年，明朝灭亡，清朝仍以北京为都，并在明城池的基础之上改造北京城。1911年，孙中山领导的辛亥革命推翻了清王朝的统治。1949年10月1日，中华人民共和国开国大典在天安门举行。从此，北京成为新中国的首都。

　　北京目前的市区规模和构架大约形成于明朝初年。市区以天安门广场为中心，东西长安街向两侧延伸，南北走向的中轴线也基本保持了原有的风貌。主要建筑均已被列为文物保护单位。今日的北京城既保存了古都的风采，又具有新时代的特征。新中国成立后，尤其是改革开放以来，北京的城市建设日新月异，向着国际化的现代都市大步迈进。

　　众多的宫殿建筑、皇家园林、宗教寺观、名人故居、古塔石刻和宏伟的现代化建筑、人文景观交相辉映，使北京成为中国名胜古迹荟集之地。本画册精选近300幅精美的图片，分为"天安门广场"、"皇家宫苑"、"文物古迹"、"京城文化"和"都市景观"五部分，向读者展示北京这座古老而又洋溢着青春活力的都市的无穷魅力。

Foreword

　　Beijing, a world-renowned ancient city of history and culture, is the capital of the People's Republic of China and the country's political, economic, cultural and transportation center. Covering an area of 16,800 square kilometers, Beijing is a super-large metropolis that has a population of 13 million. It has a semi-humid continental climate in the warm temperate zone with four distinctive seasons. Winter is cold and dry, while summer hot and humid. Spring and autumn are short. Beijing is indeed an ideal place to visit all round the year. The best seasons in Beijing are Spring and Autumn.

　　Beijing is located in the northernmost part of North China Plain, and the nature has bestowed her advantageous geographical environment and a pleasant temperate climate. As early as 500,000 years ago, the ancestors of human beings kindled the fire of ancient civilization. Some 3,000 years ago, the city emerged, being one of the first cities in world. About 800 years ago, Beijing became the national capital for the first time.

　　In the early 10th century, Khitan, a nomadic tribe in the northeast China established the Liao Dynasty, and made president Beijing the secondary capital. At the time, it was named Nanjing (Southern Capital, also known as Yanjing), because it was located at southern part of

the dynasty's territory. After more than one century, the Liao was defeated by the Jin Dynasty, which was established by Jerchen, another tribe in the northeast. In order to maintain their control over the Yellow River Valley and at the same time remain in easy contact with their base in the northeast, the Jin rulers moved their capital to the city of Nanjing in 1153, and renamed it Zhongdu (Middle Capital). In 1214, the Jin ruler was forced to move the capital to Bianjing (today's Kaifeng) by the threat of emerging power of Mongols, who captured Zhongdu the following year. In 1267, Kublai Khan issued an order to build a new city to the northwest of Zhongdu, and made it as his capital which was called Dadu (Great Capital). Four years later, he ascended the throne in the new city and established the Yuan Dynasty. With the accession of the Ming Dynasty, who defeated the Mongols in 1368, the capital temporarily shifted to present-day Nanjing by Zhu Yuanzhang, leader of the peasant rebellion and founder of the dynasty. However, Zhu Di, who guarded Beijing and became the latter Emperor Yongle, launched an interfamilial war to the capital Nanjing after Zhu Yuanzhang's death and usurped the imperial power in 1402. Since Zhu Di had been a frontier commander in Beiping for many years, he realized that Beiping was a city of strategic importance to the whole country, and a

peaceful northern boundary was of vital importance to the whole country too. In 1403, he changed his reign title to Yongle and decided to move the capital to Beijing. Thereafter, large-scale construction was carried out. Lots of buildings including city walls, palaces, temples and gardens were added, and the city was much larger than Dadu. In 1421, Zhu Di officially moved the capital to Beijing. Subsequent, post-Ming history is dominated by the rise and eventual collapse of the Manchurians — the Qing Dynasty, northerners who ruled China from Beijing from 1644. The successive Qing rulers spent a large amount of money and manpower on improving or rebuilding new pleasure grounds in and around the city on base of the Ming city. In 1911, a revolution led by Dr. Sun Yat-sen overthrew the Qing Dynasty, the last feudal dynasty of China. It was on October 1, 1949, that Chairman Mao Zedong hoisted the red flag in Tian'anmen to proclaim officially the founding of People's Republic of China. From then onwards, Beijing became the capital of the new republic.

It was in Yongle's reign that the basic city plan took shape, rigidly symmetrical, extending in squares and rectangles from the palace and inner-city grid to the suburbs, much as it is today. After liberation, with steady progress in urban development, the city walls were demolished, and smooth, wide ring roads

have been built on their foundations. Yet, parts of the old city wall and gate-tower have been preserved, so that Beijing today has retained the charms of an ancient capital city while emerging quickly as a modern metropolis. The Tian'anmen Square remains the center of Beijing, and Chang'an Boulevard has been extended, and the axial line of the city, running from south to north, is still clustered with former imperial palaces and sections of the city wall which are under the state protection as cultural treasure. Today, dramatic changes have taken place in Beijing, who is marching towards an international modern metropolis.

Numerous palace complexes, imperial gardens, temples of different religions, former residence of celebrities, ancient pagodas and stone carvings, as well as modernized buildings and new artificial tourist scenes add radiance and beauty to each other, making Beijing a land pock-marking with scenic spots and places of historical and cultural interest. In order to help domestic and overseas tourists gain a better understanding of Beijing and display the beauty and charm of the ancient yet new city, we have handpick nearly 300 exquisite pictures and compiled this album, which consists five parts: Tian'anmen Square, Imperial Palaces and Gardens, Places of Historical Interest, Beijing's Culture and Modern Attractions.

雄伟壮丽的天安门广场位于北京市中心，是中华民族的光辉标志，是首都北京的心脏，也是北京最著名的旅游胜地之一。

天安门广场得名于其北端的天安门城楼，明清时期是一处皇家禁地，由高大的宫墙围护。1911年，孙中山领导的辛亥革命推翻了清王朝的统治，天安门广场解禁。从此，广场目睹了在这里发生的幕幕历史变迁。1919年，在天安门广场爆发了反帝反封建的"五四运动"，标志着中国新民主主义革命的开端；1926年，在天安门广场集会后即爆发了震撼全国的"三·一八惨案"；1935年，爱国学生在天安门广场举行了反对帝国主义列强侵占中国领土的"一二·九运动"。1949年10月1日，毛泽东主席在天安门城楼上，向全世界庄严宣告了中华人民共和国的成立，天安门广场的历史也揭开了新的一页。

天安门广场

Tian'anmen Square

Right in the center of Beijing proper, the magnificent Tian'anmen Square is brilliant symbol of confidence and self-reliance of Chinese Nation, as well as one of the most famous attractions in Beijing.

The Tian'anmen Square is named after the imposing Tian'anmen (Gate of Heavenly Peace) Gate-tower located in its north. It used to be a forbidden area during the Ming and Qing dynasties and was surrounded by lofty palace walls on all sides. In 1911, the revolution led by Dr. Sun Yat-sen overthrew the Qing Dynasty, the last feudal dynasty of China. From then onwards, the Tian'anmen Square was opened to the public. The square is symbolically the heart of Beijing and even China, and the events it has witnessed have shaped the history of the People's Republic of China from its inception. In 1919, the epoch-making "May 4 Movement" broke out here, and the incident of March 18, 1926, and the movement of December 9, 1935 all took place in this square. On October 1 1949, Chairman Mao Zedong, standing on the Tian'anmen Gate-tower, declared to the world that the "People's Republic of China has been founded".

天安门广场
Tian'anmen Square

天安门广场占地面积44万平方米，为当今世界上最大的城市中心广场，可同时容纳100万人举行盛大的集会与庆典活动。天安门城楼雄踞于广场北端，金碧辉煌。天安门前五星红旗高高飘扬。巍峨的人民英雄纪念碑矗立于广场中央。纪念碑的南面为庄严肃穆的毛主席纪念堂。广场南端是高大典雅的正阳门（前门）城楼。这些宏大的建筑，自北而南坐落在一条中轴线上，与广场西侧的人民大会堂、东侧的国家博物馆，共同构成了一幅气势磅礴的画卷。

The Tian'anmen Square is the largest public square in the world. With a total floor space of 440,000 square meters, it accommodates up to a million people. Today, the magnificent Tian'anmen Gate Tower sits at the north, the bright Five-Star Red Flag flies high on the square, the lofty Monument to the People's Heroes dominates the center, the towering National Museum of China and the solemn Great Hall of the People to the east and west of it, as well as the dignified Chairman Mao's Memorial Hall and the elegant Zhengyangmen, sit in the south of the square. These buildings, old and new, together form a grand spectacle of tremendous momentum.

1 节日的天安门广场
Tian'anmen Square on festivals
2 俯瞰天安门广场
An Aerial Photograph of the Tian'anmen Square

天安门城楼位于广场正北，建于明永乐十五年（1417年），初名承天门，清顺治八年（1651年）改建，更名天安门。城楼坐落在巨大的条石砌成的城台之上，为重檐歇山顶式建筑，面阔九间，进深五间，朱墙黄瓦，飞金走彩，金碧辉煌，雄伟壮观。

天安门是明、清两代皇城的正门，皇帝出巡、出征、祭祀等由此门出入；每逢皇帝即位、大婚、册立皇后等大典，均在此颁布诏书。

天安门城楼内外，分别竖立有一对浑圆精美的雕龙华表。门前清澈的金水河上，跨有7座汉白玉雕栏石桥，统称外金水桥。桥两侧还设有威武的大石狮。这些装饰与天安门城楼融为一体，形成了和谐、雄浑的气势。

Tian'anmen (Gate of Heavenly Peace), a structure in a traditional Chinese architectural style, is located in the north of the square with same name. It was first constructed in 1417, the 15th year of Ming Emperor Yongle's reign, with the original name Chengtianmen (Gate of Heavenly Succession). In 1651, under the Qing Emperor Shunzhi, the gate

1 天安门城楼
  Tian'anmen Gate-tower
2 天安门城楼内景
  Interior of the Tian'anmen Gate-tower
3 天安门夜景
  Tian'anmen in night

tower was rebuilt in the original style and renamed Tian'anmen. Today it retains the basic character of the early Qing gate. 9-bayed in width and 5-bayed in depth, the gate tower has a double-eaved gable-hip roof covered with yellow glazed tiles. The structure with vermilion walls, yellow glazed tiles and golden lacquered decorations, looks splendid and magnificent.

Tian'anmen was the principal entry to the Imperial Palace during the Ming and Qing dynasties, as well as the place where state ceremonies took place. The most important one of them was the issuing of imperial edicts. Tian'anmen was also gate that the emperor and his retinue went through on their way to the altars for ritual and religious activities or for an imperial inspection tour.

Standing to the north and south of the gate are a pair of ornamental architectures called Huabiao, which were made of marble engraved with entwist-ing dragons and clouds. A stream flows in front of Tian'anmen, and is called Waijinshuihe (Outer Golden Water River), with seven marble bridges spanning over it. Additionally, two stone lions by the gate of Tian'anmen, one on each side, were meant as sentries. These decorative architectures blend with the surrounding area to complete the beautiful scenery of Tian'anmen, as well as play up a manner of harmony, gracefulness and imposingness.

人民英雄纪念碑矗立在天安门广场中心，建成于1958年。纪念碑通高37.94米，碑身正面镌刻有毛主席题写的"人民英雄永垂不朽"八个镏金大字，碑背面则是由毛主席撰文、周总理书写的碑文，东、西两侧上部刻有红星、松柏、旗帜等装饰花纹，具有"光辉永照"的含义。碑座四面共有八幅浮雕，每幅高2米，宽2～6.4米，共雕有近180个人物形象。

The Monument to the People's Heroes, standing in the center of the square, was constructed from August 1952 to May 1958. It was built in memory of thousands of martyrs who died for the revolutionary cause of the Chinese people. In the form of an obel-isk, the monument is 37.94 meters high. Its northern facade is dominated by the inscription, "Eternal Glory to the People's Heroes," in Mao Zedong's hand. On its back is an article written by Chairman Mao, but in Chinese calligraphy by the late premier Zhou Enlai. At the top of the Monument are decorated with red stars, pine trees and cy-presses, as well as wreathes of flowers includuing peony, lotus and chrys-anthemum, symbolizing the eternal glory. The lower plinth is decorated with 8 marble bas-reliefs, each being 2 meters high and 2 to 6.4 meters wide, depicting the important historic events happened in Chinese history in more than one hundred years.

4 人民英雄纪念碑
Monument to the People's Heroes

5 华表
Huabiao

天安门广场

11

毛主席纪念堂，建成于1977年，是一座富有民族特色的方形大厦。纪念堂占地面积5.7万多平方米，主体建筑，地上两层，地下一层。大厦四周环有44根八角形的花岗石高大廊柱，高高擎起黄琉璃重檐屋顶。整幢建筑的外墙均用黄色花岗岩贴面。

位于毛主席纪念堂正门之内的北大厅是举行纪念活动的场所。大厅中央是3米多高用汉白玉雕塑的毛泽东坐像，坐像背后墙上悬挂着巨幅绒绣《山河图》。北大厅之南是瞻仰厅，为纪念堂的主体，大厅正面的汉白玉墙上镶着17个镏金隶书大字"伟大的领袖和导师毛泽东主席永垂不朽"。厅内正中黑色花岗石棺床上放着水晶棺，棺内是毛主席遗体，身着灰色中山装，覆盖着鲜艳的党旗。水晶棺基座是用泰山黑色花岗石制成。棺座四周分别镶着金饰党徽、国徽、军徽和毛主席的生卒年份。南大厅为出口厅，壁上镌刻有毛主席手书《满江红》词一首。纪念堂二层为陈列室，主要陈列毛泽东主席生前的遗物，并设有电影厅，供人们一睹毛泽东等老一代无产阶级革命家的音容笑貌。

With strong national characteristics, the Chairman Mao's Memorial Hall was built in 1977 with an area of 57,000 square meters. The hall has three stories, the upper two of which are on the ground. In the four sides of the building, there are 44 octagonal granite columns, which support the yellow-glazed-tile-covered double roofs, giving a solemn atmosphere to the building. The exposed wall is faced with yellow granite.

The first floor is divided into Northern Hall, Hall of Mourning, and Southern Hall. The Northern Hall is the place where memorial activities are held, which houses a seated figure of Chairman Mao made of white marble. Behind the 3-meter-high marble status is an immense tapestry "Such a beauty is our motherland". The Hall of Mourning is the heart of the memorial hall. On the white marble wall in the front of the hall are 17 gilded characters meaning "The great leader and chairman Mao Zedong will endure forever." In the center of the hall is a black granite coffin bed, on which a crystal coffin lies. Inside the coffin, the remains of Chairman Mao wears gray suit and is covered with the red flag of the Communist Party. The base of the crystal coffin is made of black granite from Mt. Taishan, and gilded Party emblems, national emblems, army's emblems, as well as Mao Zedong's date of birth and date of death are inlaid on the four sides of the coffin. The Southern Hall leads to the exit. On the wall of the hall, a poem by Chairman Mao and in his own calligraphy is inscribed in gold inlay. It expresses his full great expectations for the country. The second floor is home to a display room, which displays things left behind by Mao Zedong, and a movie show room, in which visitors can view the demeanor of Mao Zedong and other great merits of revolutionists on the screen.

1 毛主席纪念堂
Chairman Mao's Memorial Hall

人民大会堂建于1959年，建筑面积17.2万平方米，是全国人民代表大会开会和全国人大常委会办公的地方，由万人大礼堂、宴会厅和人大办公楼三部分组成。万人大礼堂为主体建筑。礼堂平面呈扇形，进深60米，宽76米，坐席共分三层，可容万人。大会堂内有会议室、休息厅、办公室300多个，其中，全国各省、直辖市、自治区和特别行政区都有一个会议厅，装饰和陈设反映了地方和民族特色。

Built in 1959, the Great Hall of the People, covering a floor space of 172,000 square meters, is the site of the China National People's Congress meetings and provides the site for other political and diplomatic activities. It consists of three parts: a 10,000-Seat Auditorium, a banquet hall, and offices for the Standing Committee of the National People's Congress and reception halls. The 10,000-Seat Auditorium, a fan-shaped structure which is 60 meters deep and 76 meters wide, is principal building of the Hall. There are more than 300 reception rooms and conference halls of various sizes. Among them, 34 reception chambers are named after various provinces, municipalities, autonomous regions, and special administrative regions. Each is different from the other in decoration and furnishings to stress their local features.

2 香港会议厅
Hong Kong Hall

3 国宾会谈厅
State Guest Talk Hall

4 人民大会堂外景
Great Hall of the People

中国国家博物馆于 2003 年 2 月 28 日挂牌成立，在原中国历史博物馆和中国革命博物馆基础上建成，是一座以历史与艺术为主、系统展示中华民族悠久文化历史的综合性博物馆。

中国历史博物馆是中国第一座国家博物馆，前身为1912年成立的"国立历史博物馆筹备处"。1926年成立国立历史博物馆，原馆址在成贤街国子监；1959年改名中国历史博物馆，并迁入现馆址，收藏各类历史文物 30 多万件，其中一级文物近2000件。中国革命博物馆前身是中央革命博物馆筹备处，成立于1950年3月。收藏有自1840年以来，中国近现代历史文物、资料、照片等，宣传中国革命和社会主义建设历史，拥有馆藏文物 12 万多件。

The National Museum of China, based on the merger of the former National Museum of Chinese History and the National Museum of Chinese Revolution, was established on February 28, 2003. It is cur-rently being reconstructed and extended, and will gradually grow into a comprehensive museum that boasts historical, cultural, and artistic properties and showcases China's time-honored history as well as glorious and venerated culture.

The Museum of Chinese History and the Museum of Chinese Revolution share a single building complex and are arranged symmetrically. They were built in 1959 as part of the project to build 10 monumental buildings in Beijing. The National Museum of Chinese History is the first national museum in China. Its predecessor was the Preparatory Department of the National History Museum, established in 1912. Then it was set up in Beijing in the Guozijian (Imperial College) on Chengxian Street and opened to the public in 1926, when it was known simple as the Museum of History. In 1959, it was renamed National Museum of Chinese History and was moved to the curren location. In its collection, there are more than 300,000 items of various cultura relics, including nearly 2,000 items o state first-grade cultural relics. The pre decessor of the National Museum of Chi nese Revolution was the Preparatory Department of the Central Museum o Revolution, established in March 1950 In its collection, there are over 120,000 pieces of cultural and revolutionary rel ics after 1840, which introduce the Chi nese revolution as well as the socialis construction of China, including 2,224 first-grade items.

1 中国国家博物馆
   National Museum of China
2 中国国家博物馆内景
   Interior of National Museum of China

正阳门，俗称前门，位于天安门广场南缘，是明、清两代北京内城的正门。城门由城楼和箭楼两部分组成。正阳门城楼始建于明永乐十九年（1421年），占地3000多平方米，坐落在砖砌城台之上。整座城楼通高42米，在北京所有城门中最为高大。明正统四年（1439年），为了加强京师的防御能力，在正阳门外添建箭楼，形制与城楼相同，上下共四层，东、西、南三面墙上辟有射孔。它是内城九门中惟一箭楼开门洞的城门，一直被视为老北京的象征。正阳门箭楼于1990年开放，四层均辟为展厅。此外，明、清时期城楼与箭楼之间有一个巨大的瓮城，南北长108米，东西宽88.6米，1914年拆除。

"Nine inside, seven outside, four in the Imperial City" is a phrase that's been used by Beijing residents since the Ming Dynasty. More explicitly, it means that there are four gates to the Imperial City, seven to the Outer City and nine to the Inner City, among which the nine gates of the Inner City, centered by Zhengyangmen (South-Facing Gate), were the most important gates.

The Zhengyangmen, located southern end of the Tian'anmen Square, was the front entrance to the Inner City of Beijing during the Ming and Qing dynasties. Popularly known as Qianmen (Front Gate), it comprises of a gate-tower and an archery tower. 42 meters in height, the gate-tower was first built in 1421 and was the largest of all city gates of old Beijing. To strengthen defense works of the capital, a fortress-like archery tower was added in 1439. Architecturally, it is similar in shape to the gate-tower, except that it has many embrasures in the walls of east, west and south which enabled soldiers to shoot arrows. It was the only archery tower that had openings among all gates to the Inner City, and had been taken as the symbol of Beijing by the older generation of Beijingers. The archery tower was opened to the public in 1990, and converted into a four-storied exhibiting venue. In the old days the two structures were linked with a walled-in enclosure, known as wengcheng (urn walls), which was 108 meters from south to north and 88.6 meters from east to west. It was demolished in 1914.

3 **正阳门城楼**
   Zhengyangmen Gate-tower

4 **箭楼**
   Archery Tower

5 **正阳门及箭楼**
   Double-gate System of Zhengyangmen

北京是享誉世界的历史文化名城，也是著名的古都。公元1153年，中国东北少数民族女真建立金朝，将北京定为都城，称为"中都"，开始了北京城的建都历史。此后的元、明、清三代均以北京为都，并在前朝的基础上大规模改造都城。直至1911年，孙中山领导的辛亥革命推翻了清王朝的统治，中国最后一个封建王朝溃亡，北京作为帝都的历史也到此结束。

金中都、元大都、明、清北京城，800多年绵延不绝的都城历史不仅让北京积淀了一份厚重的文化沧桑，更使她拥有了众多的皇家遗迹。金碧辉煌的故宫、恢宏神秘的天坛、优美典雅的颐和园和秀丽多姿的北海公园是这些皇家建筑的杰出代表。这些宝贵的文化遗产，充分展示了中华民族高超的智慧和非凡的创造力。它们是北京作为世界历史文化名城的精华所在，也是北京独具特色和魅力的瑰宝。

皇家宫苑

Imperial Palaces and Gardens

Beijing is a world-renowned ancient city of history and culture, as well as a well-known ancient capital. Her history as a national capital starts from 1153 when rulers of the Jin Dynasty, established by Jerchen, a tribe in the northeast China, moved their capital to this city. At the time, it was called Zhongdu (Middle Capital). Ever since then, Beijing's position of a national capital maintained though some minor changes under different names in different dynasties down to the present day with only minor interruptions. The successive three dynasties — Yuan, Ming and Qing — all devoted great efforts to the construction, reinforcement, and development of Beijing on base of the former dynasty, during the spanning of more than 800 years. In 1911, a revolution led by Dr. Sun Yat-sen overthrew the Qing Dynasty, which also marked the end of Beijing's history as the capital of feudal dynasty.

A long history has left numerous famous imperial architectural compounds, including the magnificent Palace Museum, the mysterious Temple of Heaven, the graceful Summer Palace and the beautiful Beihai Park. All these precious treasures are outstanding representatives of imperial architectural compound of Beijing, and have demonstrated the high wisdom and extraordinary creativity of the Chinese nation. They have formed the essence of a city of history and culture as well as the uniqueness and the charm of Beijing.

故宫博物院
Palace Museum

故宫博物院坐落于北京市中心，旧称紫禁城，是世界上现存规模最大、最完整的古代木结构建筑群。这座宫城规模宏大、气势磅礴，集中体现了中国古代建筑艺术的优秀传统和独特风格，是中国古建的经典之作。1987年，联合国教科文组织将故宫作为文化遗产项目列入《世界遗产名录》。

故宫始建于明永乐四年（公元1406年），历时14年建成，为明、清两代帝王处理朝政和居住的皇宫，先后有24位皇帝（明朝14帝，清朝10帝）在此统治中国近500年。故宫总面积达72万平方米，建筑面积15万平方米，共有殿宇楼阁8704间，中轴布局，左右对称，前朝后廷，殿院递进。总体平面呈长方形，周围环绕有10米多高的城墙，墙外是52米宽、3800米长的护城河。宫墙四隅建有四座精巧玲珑的角楼，均为9梁18柱72脊式的三层楼阁，使故宫自成防御体系，是一座名副其实的"城中之城"。故宫的建筑，继承和发扬了中国历代宫殿建筑的传统工艺，为营建这组巍峨浩大的建筑群，征用了当时全国知名的工匠10多万人，以及民夫、军役百余万人。建筑材料也极为讲究，均从全国各地精心挑选，运至北京。

故宫虽经明、清两代帝王多次重修和增建，但其建筑基本保持着初建时布局。宫城的内部格局分为外朝和内廷，主要建筑依次坐落在纵横南北的中轴线上，主体突出，层次分明，既增加了其雄伟恢宏的气势，又突出了皇权至高无上的思想。外朝的主体建筑为三大殿，即太和殿、中和殿和保和殿，是皇帝举行大典、召见群臣和行使权力的地方。内廷是皇帝处理政务以及皇室成员居住、游玩、奉神之处，主体建筑有乾清宫、交泰殿、坤宁宫，即后三宫，以及东六宫、西六宫、养心殿、御花园等。

故宫博物院藏有艺术珍品及明、清宫廷历史文物90多万件，其中有许多为国宝级文物。现设有青铜器馆、陶瓷馆、明、清工艺美术馆、钟表馆、绘画馆、珍宝馆等供游人观赏。

Lying at the center of Beijing City, the Palace Museum is much better known in the West as the Forbidden City. The largest wooden cluster in existence in the world today, the Palace Museum was the symbolic heart of the capital, the empire and (so the emperors believed) the world. This magnificent, solemn and palatial complex is a masterpiece of traditional Chinese architectural works. In 1987, the United Nations Educational, Scientific and Cultural Organization (UNESCO) added it on the List of World Heritage.

做工精细的门
Elaborate Palace Gate

皇 家 宫 苑 · 故 宫

Construction of the Forbidden City began in 1406, the 4th year of Ming Emperor Yongle's reign, and was completed fourteen years later. During the Ming and Qing dynasties, a spanning of nearly 500 years, 24 emperors, 14 of the Ming and 10 of the Qing, lived and exercised their supreme power over the nation from here. From within, the emperors, the Sons of Heaven, issued commands with absolute authority to their millions of subjects. Occupying an area of 72 hectares, it is rectangular in shape. Scattered across the palace city are 8,704 rooms totaling about 150,000 square meters. The palaces are fully walled on four sides by 10-meter-high walls, 7.236 kilometers in circumference. Outside the walls a 52-meter-wide moat, lengthening 3.8 kilometers, surrounds the city. There are unique and delicately structured corner towers on each of the four corners of the curtain wall, affording views over both the palace and the city outside. All these make the Forbidden City "a miniature city of cities".

The Forbidden City had been repaired and rebuilt many times during some 500 years, but its basic form and layout remains in the original state. It is divided into two parts: the Outer Court and the Inner Court. All structures were arranged symmetrically in a hierarchical order along the central axis, showing breathtaking magnificence and

1

皇
家
宫
苑
·
故
宫

majestic imperial manner, as well as demonstrating the supremacy of imperial power. The Outer Court was where the emperor held grand ceremonies, summoned ministers and exercised his supreme power over the country. Major structures are the Three Grand Halls: Taihedian (Hall of Supreme Harmony), Zhonghedian (Hall of Complete Harmony) and Baohedian (Hall of Preserved Harmony). Aligned with the central axis, the Three Rear Palaces — Qianqinggong (Palace of Celestial Purity), Jiaotaidian (Hall of Celestial and Terrestrial Union), and Kunninggong (Palace of Terrestrial Tranquility) — are core structures of the Inner Court, where the emperor and his family lived,

amused and dedicated the gods of different religions. Other principal structures include the Six Eastern and Western Palaces, Yangxindian (Hall of Mental Cultivation), Imperial Garden, and so on.

The Forbidden City takes pride in its precious collections of more than 900,000 cultural and art objects, many of which are state relics. There are exhibition halls, where visitors can admire bronze ware, pottery, arts and crafts of Ming and Qing dynasties, clocks, paintings, carvings, and other precious treasures.

1 故宫雪景
The Forbidden City after Snow

午门,是紫禁城的南门,始建于明永乐十八年（1420年）。东西北三面城台相连,,环抱一个方形广场。城台之上建有崇楼五座,北面门楼,面阔九间,重檐黄瓦庑殿顶,两侧城台上各建有两座方形重檐四角攒尖顶楼阁,各楼之间有明廊相连。五楼翘檐耸脊,宛如凌空展翅的飞鸟,故俗称五凤楼。明、清两代,凡大规模出征、凯旋、献俘、颁布历书等重大活动都在此举行仪式。

午门正中辟有三门,两侧各有掖门一座,为"明三暗五"形式。从午门出入紫禁城有严格的规定。清朝时,当中的正门平日只有皇帝才能出入;皇帝大婚时,皇后可以进一次;殿试考中状元、榜眼、探花的三人可以从此门走出一次。平时文武百官走东侧门,宗室王公走西侧门,大朝日子则文官东、武官西,由东西拐角的掖门出入。

The Wumen (Meridian Gate), the south entrance to the Forbidden City, was first built in 1420, the 18th reign year under Ming Emperor Yongle. This gate is surmounted by five towers, also known as the Wufenglou (Five-Phoenix Tower). The main gate-tower sitting in the front is a 9-bayed structure with a double-eaved hip roof covered with yellow glazed tiles, flanking which are two massive wings, forming a huge square. On each wing are two square towers covered with double-eaved pyramid roofs. They are connected by covered galleries. During the Ming and Qing dynasties, such grand ceremonies as dispatching the generals into fields of war, accepting prisoners of war, celebrating victories and announcing the new calendar for the following year, were held here.

The Wumen actually has a total of five openings: three on its facade, which could be seen directly, and two on the sides. Everyone who entered the Forbidden City had to observe strict rules concerning the use of the Wumen in the past. During the Qing Dynasty, entering through the central opening was the emperor's exclusive privilege, while his empress was allowed to go through the opening once on her wedding day. As a special honor, the three finalists who achieved the highest awards in the national examinations presided over by the emperor, would be permitted to strut through the central opening after receiving emperor's interview. High-ranking civil and military officials went through the side gate on the east and princes and royal family members on the west. Yet when went to court, the civil officials used the further side gate at the east corner while the military officers used the west.

1 俯瞰午门
A Bird's Eye View of Wumen

2 午门
Wumen

太和殿，俗称金銮殿，是三大殿中最为庄严、崇伟的一座。大殿建在三层汉白玉栏杆环绕的台基上，重檐庑殿顶上覆黄琉璃瓦，面阔十一间，进深五间，连台通高35.05米，总面积2300多平方米，是中国现存最大的木结构建筑。明、清两代，皇帝即位、大婚、册立皇后以及元旦赐宴和命将出征等大典均在此举行。

皇宫正殿太和殿是朝廷举行重大仪式的地方，为显示皇权的至高无上，大殿建筑得格外巍峨雄壮。殿内84根楠木大柱，支撑着182根梁枋组成的梁架，承托起金碧辉煌四面坡形的殿顶。殿内地面用4718块"金砖"铺就，至今仍平整如镜、油润光滑。殿内正中基台之上，放置皇帝九龙金漆宝座，宝座后为金漆楠木雕龙屏风。大殿从屋面装饰到内外檐彩画，以及藻井天花，编饰龙纹、龙雕，表现出皇帝贵为真龙天子，至高无上的权利和地位。

皇帝宝座由龙椅和座基组成，象征皇权的金漆雕龙椅高踞于有七层台级的基台上，周围陈设华美。当皇帝登上宝座时，他比跪在广场的大臣足足高出11米。这种设计极大地突出了皇权的至高无上，在殿内营造出一种神秘的气氛。太和殿藻井内饰浑金蟠龙，蟠龙口衔轩辕宝镜，以示皇帝是中国始祖轩辕黄帝的正统继承者。

3 太和门广场
Taihemen Square

4 太和门广场雪景
Taihemen Square after Snow

5 太和殿
Taihedian

皇家宫苑·故宫

Taihedian, also known as Jinluandian (literally, the Golden Carriage Palace), is the most magnificent among the Three Grand Halls. Standing on a richly balustraded three-storied marble terrace, this single palace reaches as high as 35.05 meters. It is 11-bayed in width and 5-bayed in depth, covering an area of 2,300 square meters, which made it the largest timbered structure extant in China. Having a double-eaved hip roof covered with yellow glazed tiles, the Taihedian was used to held grand ceremony when a new emperor ascended the throne. Celebrations also marked emperor's birthday, wedding ceremony, empress's conferment and other important occasions such as the Chinese New Year and the dispatch of generals into fields of war.

Taihedian used to be the place that grand ceremonies were held, so the magnificent and imposing hall showcased the supreme power of feudal emperors. 84 giant nanmu pillars support the structural frame of beam consisting of 182 beams and hewn timbers totally, as well as its splendid four-slope roof. The floor is paved with 4,718 special bricks known as "Golden Bricks" which were fired long and then polished by being soaked in tungoil. As a symbol of imperial power, the sandalwood throne, standing on a high platform, sits in the center of the hall, behind which is a golden-lacquered nanmu screen carved with dragons. The Taihedian is richly decorated with dragon images on the throne, pillars, eaves, walls, roofs, etc., giving an aura of solemnity and mystery, and demonstrating the supreme power of the emperor, the Son of Heaven.

The imperial throne in the center of the Taihedian comprises of the throne and its base. The gold-lacquered throne with carvings of dragon, symbolizing the supreme imperial power, is sitting on a seven-floor base. The throne is so high that when the emperor seated on his

1 太和殿内景
Interior of Taihedian

2 太和殿藻井
Caisson of Taihedian

throne, his feet were 11 meters above the heads of his officials. Such design intensifies the imposing dignity of the ruler and surrounds the throne and building with an atmosphere of mystery and awesomeness. In the middle of the ceiling is design of a coiled golden dragon playing with a huge pearl. The pearl in dragon's mouth was called Precious Mirror of Xuanyuan (Emperor Huangdi's name). It symbolized that the emperor was the legitimate successor of Emperor Huangdi. It was believed that if anyone who was not the descendant of the Emperor Huangdi usurped the throne, the pearl would drop down and strike him dead.

中和殿位于太和殿之后,是一座形制特殊的宫殿,初名华盖殿。大殿高27米,方檐圆顶,深阔各五间,殿内顶部的雕镂彩绘极其精美。明、清时期,当太和殿举行大典时,皇帝先停辇在中和殿小憩,并接受大典中执事官员的参拜。每年祭祀天坛、地坛、太庙时,皇帝在这里阅读祭文;在先农坛举行亲耕礼之前,皇帝要在此殿内阅看祭文和亲耕时用的农具。清代规定每十年纂修一次皇帝的宗谱,纂修好以后,进呈皇帝审阅的仪式,也在中和殿举行。

保和殿是外朝最后一座大殿。大殿平面呈长方形,重檐歇山顶上覆黄琉璃瓦。在明代,此殿是举行册立皇后、皇太子等大典前,皇帝更衣的地方。清朝时,皇帝在此殿赐宴额驸之父,以及有官职的家属。

每逢除夕、上元节,皇帝亦在此宴请外藩、王公及一、二品大臣。此外,自乾隆皇帝始,每科殿试均在保和殿举行。

Standing behind Taihedian, the Zhonghedian is a square hall initially known as Huagaidian (Hall of Canopy). Its single-eaved pyramid roof is covered with yellow glazed tiles and crowned by a gilded ball in the center. It served as a place of rest for the emperor on his way to Taihedian. It was here that the emperor consulted with their religious ministers. Each year prior to his departure for sacrificial rites at the Tiantan (Temple of Heaven), Ditan (Altar of the Earth) and Taimiao (Ancestral Temple), the emperor would read prayers here; before going to the Xiannongtan (Altar of Creator of Agriculture), the emperor would inspect the seeds and farming tools to be used during the ceremony. During the Qing dynasty the imperial genealogy was revised every ten years. A special ceremony would be conducted in Zhonghedian while the revision of imperial genealogy was done.

The Baohedian stands at the northern end of the three-storied marble terrace. Similar in style but somewhat smaller

1 太和殿雪景
Snowy Scene of Taihedian

2 中和殿

Zhonghedian

than the Taihedian, this hall has a double-eaved gable-hip roof covered with yellow glazed tiles. Ming emperor usually changed into his ritual garment here prior to the ceremonial installation of an empress or crown prince. During the Qing Dynasty, the hall was used to hold imperial banquets. The emperor would entertain princess's bridegroom and his father together with their relatives who served the imperial government. Each year, on the eve of the New Year, banquets would be held to feast and honor provincial governors, Mongolian princes, civil and military officials. Beginning from Qianlong's reign, the final stage of the Palace Examination, which was the highest level of the nation-wide imperial examination system, was transferred from the Taihedian to Baohe-dian.

In the center of the stairway outside the north gate of Baohedian, is a huge marble relief of nine vivid dragons playing on waves and in clouds. Weighing about 250 tons, it is the largest stone carving in the Palace Museum.

3 云龙大石雕
  Huge Marble Ramp Carved with Cloud and Dragon Design
4 保和殿内景
  Interior of Baohedian
5 中和殿和保和殿
  Zhonghedian and Baohedian

皇家宫苑 · 故宫

乾清宫是内廷的正殿，其形制和陈设均与太和殿相同，只是规模略小。大殿高20米，面阔九间，重檐庑殿顶，坐落在一层汉白玉台基上。台基上的甬道直通乾清门，两旁有汉白玉的雕栏，金殿玉阶交相辉映。

明朝和清初，乾清宫是皇帝的寝宫。明代的十四个皇帝和清代的顺治、康熙两个皇帝，都以乾清宫为寝宫，在这里居住并处理日常政务。清雍正以后，皇帝的寝宫移至养心殿，这里专门用来举行内廷典礼、召见官员和接见外国使臣。每逢元旦、元宵、端午、中秋、重阳、冬至、除夕、万寿等节日，也在此举行内朝礼和赐宴。在清代，乾清宫还是皇帝死后停放灵柩的地方。不论皇帝死于何处，都要先把灵柩运到乾清宫停放几天，按照规定的仪式祭奠以后，再停到景山寿皇殿等处，最后选定日期正式出殡，入葬皇陵。

乾清宫殿内正中座台上，设有皇帝宝座及御案，四周陈设香炉、香亭、仙鹤饰物。宝座整体贴金，并镶嵌红、绿宝石，扶手和靠背金龙缠绕，尤为精美。宝座上方匾额上的"正大光明"四字为清顺治皇帝手书，匾额后就是自雍正帝起置放建储匣的地方。

中国历代封建王朝的皇位继承，基本上采取公开建储的办法，在位的皇帝大多将皇长子册立为皇太子，以承袭帝位。清

朝初年也遵循历代帝制。雍正即位后，对皇子之间争夺皇权有着深刻的体会。他吸取历代封建王朝公开建储的经验教训，创立了秘密建储制度。其做法是皇帝将选定的储君的名字写在纸上，一式两份，一份封存在建储匣中，安放在乾清宫"正大光明"匾后，另一份藏在皇帝身边。皇帝去世后，由顾命大臣启封、并核对两份遗诏，无误后宣布皇位继承人。

在乾清宫前露台两侧，有两座石台，石台上各设一座鎏金铜亭，叫江山社稷金殿，又叫金亭子。金殿每面安设四扇隔扇门，重檐，上层檐为圆形攒尖，上安宝顶，象征江山社稷、国家政权都掌握在皇帝手中。

The Qianqinggong, core structure of the Inner Court, is a smaller version of the Taihedian. As it was deemed inferior to the Taihedian, everything within it is smaller than similar items in the superior palace. 20 meters in height and 9-bayed in width, this hall has a double-eaved hip roof and was built on a white marble terrace. Flanked by carved marble balustrades, a paved path leads straightly to the Qianqingmen (Gate of Celestial Purity). The golden palace and jade-like steps add radiance and beauty to each other.

It was the palace where all emperors of the Ming and two emperors of the Qing — Shunzhi and Kangxi — used to live and handle daily affairs. Qing Emperor Yongzheng was the first emperor to move his living quarters to Yangxindian (Hall of Mental Cultivation). This building was then used as an audience chamber where the emperor held ceremonies and received envoys from vassal states who presented their tributes to the emperor. Foreign ambassadors were received here. Imperial banquets were also held here on Chinese traditional festivals including the New Year, Lantern Festival, Dragon Boat Festival, Mid-Autumn Festival, Double Ninth Festival, Winter Solstice, and the emperor's birthday. Moreover, in the Qing dynasty, no matter where the emperor died, his coffin would be placed in this palace for a few days for memorial ceremonies. Later the coffin would be moved to Shouhuangdian (Hall of Imperial Longevity) or Guandedian (Hall of Morals Observation) in today's Jingshan (Prospect Hill) Park, and then buried in the mausoleum on a selected day.

In the center of the Qianqinggong, the throne and imperial table are on a raised dais, surrounded by cloisonne decorations of incense burners, incense pavilions, and red-crowned cranes. The throne is entirely covered with gold and inlaid with red and green gems, and its armrests and back are carved with coiling golden dragons. Over the throne hangs a plaque engraved with four Chi-

1 乾清宫内景
  Interior of Qianqinggong
2 雨中的乾清宫
  Rainy Scene of Qianqinggong
3 乾清宫内的龙椅
  Throne in Qianqinggong

nese characters written by Emperor Shunzhi, which mean "Be open and aboveboard". From the time of Emperor Yongzheng, the name of each crown prince would be written on the imperial edict and placed in a box behind this plaque.

According to the traditional rule of succession, the imperial throne would always be passed to the legal wife's eldest son of the emperor, and the emperor would announce name of the crown prince publicly before his death. Understanding the bred fierce conflicts frequently occurred among the imperial princes, Qing Emperor Yongzheng abolished the system, which had been used for thousands of years in China. The name of the successor to the throne was no longer announced publicly for the reason of security. The emperor would write the name of his successor on duplicate documents, and a copy would be placed in a box behind the plaque of "Be open and above-board", the other copy being retained by the emperor. The box was opened only after the emperor passed away. Only if the name on each document was the same would the designated prince take the crown upon the death of the emperor. This box was used to store the imperial testamentary edict of designating crown prince.

In front of the Qianqinggong, there is a small miniature pavilion on a marble terrace on each side. They are collectively known as the Jiangshan (national territory) Shejing (god of the land and grain) Halls, or Golden Pavilions. Square in shape, each of them is installed with four-leaf door and has a double-eaved pyramid roof — the upper is round and the lower is square. They together represent the supreme imperial power.

1 军机处
   Office of the Privy Council
2 江山社稷亭
   Jiangshan Sheji Hall
3 交泰殿内景
   Interior of Jiaotaidian

3

交泰殿位于乾清宫和坤宁宫之间，含天地交合、安康美满之意。此殿平面呈正方形，单檐四角攒尖顶，铜鎏金宝顶，四面辟门，形制与中和殿相同。殿内正中设皇后宝座，上悬康熙御书"无为"匾。左侧置铜壶滴漏，右侧置大自鸣钟。清代每年元旦、冬至、千秋（皇后的生日）三大节日，皇后在此受贺。每年春季去先蚕坛祭祀前，皇后需来此处阅视采桑工具。此外，乾隆皇帝亲自考正、选定25方用途不一的御用宝玺存在交泰殿内，统称为"二十五宝"，寓意大清江山长绵永固。

Sitting between the Qianqinggong and Kunninggong, the Jiaotaidian is smaller in size than the Zhonghedian, although they look the same in style. As its name implies, it symbolizes harmonious mergence between the heaven and earth, as well as the happy marriage of the emperor and empress. This square structure has an opening on each side and a single-eaved pyramid roof topped by a gilt bronze crown. In the center of

Jiaotaidian is the throne of empress. The two Chinese characters inscribed on the plaque by Emperor Kangxi hanging above the throne are "Wu Wei", meaning to govern the country by noninterference, a Taoist philosophy. Standing in the hall are water clock on the left and chiming clock on the right. It was here that empress received formal greetings from all the concubines, princesses and maids on New Year's Day, Winter Solstice and her birthday. Empress would inspect preparations before she went to preside over memorial ceremonies for the Silkworm God and practice sericulture. Since the reign of Qianlong, imperial seals used by former emperors were kept in this hall. No seals were allowed out of the hall without the prior consent of the emperor. The presently kept 25 seals were chose by Qianlong to stop the confusion of the seals' use and to determine the specific number of seals. The Number 25, total of 1, 3, 5, 7, 9, was regarded as a heavenly number, which denote the wish of Qianlong for the Qing dynasty to last for ever.

坤宁宫是内廷最后一座大殿,面阔九间,进深三间。明代,坤宁宫是皇后的寝宫。清代自雍正开始皇帝从乾清宫迁居养心殿,皇后也不再以坤宁宫为寝宫。

清顺治十二年(1655年)重建时,按满族习俗将西端改建为祭神的场所,例如将正门开在偏东的一间,改菱花窗格为直条窗格,殿内明间和西部南、西、北三面为环形大炕,作为祭神之处。坤宁宫祭神,除日祭、月祭外,每年的正月初和春秋两季还举行三次大祭。

坤宁宫的东暖阁是皇帝大婚时的洞房。帝后举行婚礼后在此居住三日,然后回各自的寝宫。

Kunninggong, 9-bayed in width and 3-bayed in depth, is the last major palace in the Inner Court. It is the only example of Manchurian architecture in the Forbidden City and was the residential palace of the empress during the Ming and early Qing dynasties. When the Emperor Yongzheng shifted his imperial bedroom from Qian-qinggong to Yangxindian, the empress also changed her living quarters.

During its renovation in 1655, the 12th year of Emperor Shunzhi's reign, it was altered in layout according to Manchurian customs, and the Western Warmth Chamber was used to pay homage to the gods of Shamanism. Rhombus-shaped window lattices were replaced by mullions; a trinity *kang* was arranged against south, west and north walls in the front chamber, which was used to pay homage to gods. Besides daily and monthly sacrificial rites, three grand ceremonies would be held in the first lunar month, spring and autumn.

The Eastern Warmth Chamber was emperor's nuptial chamber in the Qing dynasty. By law the emperor had to spend the first three nights of his marriage here with empress, and then they went back to their respective bedrooms.

1 *铜壶滴漏*
  Water Clock
2 *后宫鸟瞰*
  A Superb Panorama of the Inner Court
3 *坤宁宫内景*
  Interior of Kunninggong

御花园东西长130米，南北宽90米，平面呈规整的长方形。全园的建筑物按中、东、西三路布置，20余座形态各异的建筑，皆按主次相辅，左右对称的格局排列配置，其间点缀着苍松翠柏、奇花异木、水池叠石等，在庄严整齐之中，力求变化，富有浓厚的宫廷气氛。园内的中心建筑为钦安殿，内供道教玄武大帝。其他主要建筑有东路的堆秀山、浮碧亭、万春亭、绛雪轩等，和西路的延晖阁、澄瑞亭、千秋亭等。东、西两路的建筑虽然布局对称，但是其形状、色彩、装饰皆有差异，使观者毫无雷同之感。

Standing at the northernmost tip of the central axis is the Imperial Garden, which is 130 meters long and 90 meters wide. The garden was laid out along three axes, and 20-odd architectural structures of different appearances are arranged symmetrically in hierarchical order, dotted with rare flowers and trees, pond and layered rocks. From the neat layout, the architect sought to use diverse forms of buildings and their supplements to play

up the imposing royal manner, and to exhibit densely characteristics of garden as well. The Qin'andian (Hall of Imperial Peace), core building in the garden, was dedicated to Taoist God, Xuanwu Dadi. Principal buildings on the eastern axis are Duixiushan (Gathering Beauty Hill), Fubiting (Jade-Green Floating Pavilion), Wanchunting (Pavilion of Ten Thousand Springs), and Jiangxuexuan (House of Crimson Snow); on the western axis are Yanhuige (Pavilion of Sustaining Sunshine), Chengruiting (Pavilion of Auspicious Clarity) and Qianqiuting (Pavilion of One Thousand Autumns). Though similar in layout, the two groups of buildings vary in shapes, colors and decorations, looking totally different.

1 堆秀山
  Duixiushan
2 御花园
  Imperial Garden
3 连枝柏
  Consort Cypresses

养心殿位于内廷西路，自雍正始成为清代皇帝的寝宫。养心殿为工字形殿，前后殿有一穿堂相连。前殿为理政之处，殿内设有宝座、御案，宝座后设有书橱，内藏历代皇帝治国经验教训等记载与书籍等。后殿为寝宫。

养心殿前殿的东暖阁，曾是西太后（慈禧）和东太后（慈安）在同治和光绪皇帝年幼时垂帘听政的地方。慈安于光绪初年去世，此后慈禧独揽大权。当时小皇帝坐于前座，慈禧坐于后座，两座之间由一道纱帘隔开。所有的决策都由纱帘后的慈禧作出。现在这里的陈设，仍是当时的场景。

The Yangxindian stands south to the Six Western Palaces in the Inner Court. From Qing Emperor Yongzheng's ruling time onwards, it was resided by emperors. An I-shaped structure, the Yangxindian consists of the front chamber and the rear chamber, linked by a hallway. The front chamber was where emperor conducted official business. The emperor's throne and table are in the center of the hall. Behind it are a screen and bookshelves on both sides, keeping

books on the experiences and lessons that the preceding emperors of various dynasties had drawn in ruling the country. The rear chamber was where emperor lived.

It was in the Eastern Warmth Chamber of Yangxindian that Cixi and Ci'an attended to state affairs sitting behind a curtain when Tongzhi and Guangxu were young. When Xianfeng died, the two dowager empresses had allies and seized control of the government. Since Empress Dowager Ci'an seldom took part in the court affairs, Empress Dowager Cixi was the real monarch, who ruled China for 48 years. Although the emperor was just a child, the empresses couldn't rule openly; they had to go through the little boy. A screen was set up behind the boy's throne. When government officials delivered their reports to the emperor, Cixi and Ci'an listened and told him what to say in return. Dutifully the young emperor parroted her words. The chamber is displayed as it was in Cixi's time: two thrones setting here were separated by a gauze curtain.

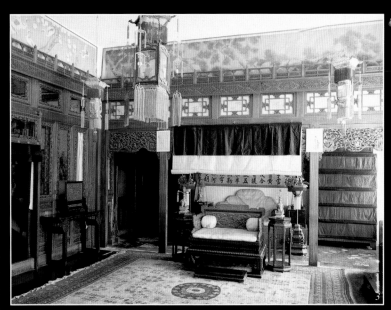

储秀宫原名寿昌宫，为明代嫔妃居住处。清代屡次重修，后妃均可居住。居于此处的后妃中，最为著名的是慈禧太后。清光绪十年（1884年），为贺慈禧太后50岁寿辰大规模改造，将翊坤宫后殿打通为穿堂殿，连通两宫院落，并在殿外增设铜雕龙、鹿。储秀宫最后的主人是末代皇帝溥仪的正妻婉容。

The Chuxiugong, initially known as Shouchanggong (Palace of Longevity and Prosperity), was resided by imperial concubines during the Ming Dynasty. The Qing emperors rebuilt it several times, and changed it into the dwelling of both empresses and concubines. The most noted hostess who lived here was Cixi. To celebrate her 50th birthday in 1884,

Cixi had the palace reconstructed extensively. Rear hall of Yikungong (Palace of the Queen Consort) was converted into a lobby, so the two palaces were linked. Bronze sculptures of dragon and deer were placed in front of the palace. The last hostess of Chuxiugong was Wanrong, "empress" of the last emperor, Puyi.

1 养心殿内景
Interior of Yangxindian

2 养心门
Yangxinmen

3 养心殿东暖阁
Eastern Warmth Chamber of Yangxindian

4 储秀宫内景
Interior of Chuxiugong

皇家宫苑·故宫

1

紫禁城城垣的四角，各建有一座结构相同的角楼。角楼高27.5米，三重檐，楼顶檐脊参差相叠，楼体朱碧相映；各有9梁，18柱，72脊。这四座角楼是供守卫宫城的兵士出望、警戒用的。

At four corners of the Forbidden City are four corner towers. Overlooking both the palace and the city outside, they served for defensive purpose. Each of the corner tower, 27.5 meters in height, consists of 9 roof beams, 18 pillars and 72 ridges, and has a cross gable-hip roof, which was covered with yellow glazed tiles and topped by a gilded bronze crown.

1 夹道
  A Passageway in the Forbidden City
2 角楼
  Corner Tower
3 角楼及护城河
  Corner Tower and the Moat

2

3

皇家宫苑·故宫

神武门是紫禁城的北门，始建于明永乐十八年，初名玄武门。清代康熙年间，因避讳康熙帝名玄烨，改称神武门。城台辟有门洞3券，台上建有门楼，面阔七间，进深三间，重檐庑殿顶。门楼上原设钟、鼓，为明清时报时所用。明代由更鼓房的太监按时依数或击鼓，或敲钟。清代这项差事由銮仪卫校卫担任。

作为皇宫后门的神武门，是后妃或皇室人员出入皇宫的专用门。皇帝出外巡幸经由午门而出，但是，随行的嫔妃必须由神武门出宫，不过皇帝从行宫或郊外御园回宫，可以由神武门入。清朝，应选秀女的女子由神武门入宫，接受挑选。

The Shenwumen (Gate of Divine Might) is the north gate of the Forbidden City, which was first built in 1420, the 18th year of Ming Emperor Yongle's reign. It was originally called Xuanwumen (Black Tortoise Gate)in the Ming Dynasty. During the Qing Emperor Kangxi's reign, to avoid coincidental association with his name, Xuanye, which was considered a taboo at that time, the name of gate was changed into present name, Shenwumen.

The gate has three openings and an imposing tower, which is 7-bayed in width and 3-bayed in depth, and covered by a multi-eaved hip roof. Housed in its tower are bells and drums which were beaten in the morning and in the evening respectively to mark time. During the Ming, the work was done by eunuchs, while the members of Luanyiwei (Department of Imperial Insignias) were in charge of it in the Qing Dynasty.

According to rules, the Shenwumen was used for empress, imperial concubines and royal family members. When the emperor made an imperial inspection tour, he went out through the Wumen, however, the entourage of his consorts had to leave the imperial palace from Shenwumen. As a matter of fact, the emperor sometimes went back the imperial palace from this gate when he finished his tours or holidays. Also, the candidates of Beauties would enter the palace through the gate.

1 神武门
Shenwumen

北海公园
Beihai Park

　　北海公园位于故宫西侧，主要由北海湖和琼华岛组成，总面积68万平方米，水域广阔，占全园面积的一半以上。这里原是辽、金、元、明、清5个封建王朝的皇家宫苑，为世界上建筑最早、保存最完整的古典皇家园林。

　　最早的北海只是一处普通的水域，水中有岛名"瑶屿"，辽代在此建有瑶屿行宫。金代统治者又在这里进一步开浚湖泊、叠土成山，作为金中都东北郊外的苑囿行宫。岛屿改称"琼华岛"，岛上建瑶光殿、广寒殿，又从汴梁(今开封)移来艮岳花石堆叠假山，北海便初具规模。到了元代，元世祖以琼华岛为中心修建元大都城，琼华岛及其所在的湖泊被划入皇城，赐名万寿山、太液池。这里便由苑囿行宫变为皇城内的帝王宫苑。明永乐十八年(1420年)，明朝正式迁都北京，万寿山、太液池成为紫禁城西面的御苑，称西苑。明代向南开拓水面，形成三海的格局。清朝承袭明代的西苑，顺治年间，在广寒殿旧址建喇嘛塔(今白塔)和永安寺等，改万寿山为白塔山；乾隆时期对北海进行大规模的改建，大兴土木长达30年，奠定了此后的规模和格局。

　　北海公园是中国古典园林的艺术杰作，它继承了中国历代的造园传统，博采各地造园技艺所长，总体布局仿照神话中的"一池三山"格局。建筑布局则以琼华岛上的白塔为中心。白塔和团城由永安大石桥连接形成一条南北轴线。琼华岛四周散布的数十座殿堂亭台均围绕这条轴线而建。北海湖的东、北两岸设有多组建筑，或临水而立，或隐没绿林，风格各异，与自然山水和谐地融合在一起，虽由人作，宛若天成。

　　Located west to the Forbidden City, the Beihai Park consists primarily of the Qionghuadao (Jade-Flowery Islet) and Beihai (North Sea) Lake. The whole park has an area of over 68 hectares, with a water area that covers more than half of the entire park. Being the former imperial palace of successive feudal dynasties including Liao, Jin, Yuan, Ming and Qing, it is the oldest and best-preserved classical imperial garden in the world.

　　Early in the 10th century, the Liao dynasty, a secondary imperial palace and an island were built here, called Yaoyu (Jade Islet). When the Jin took over, the rulers of the dynasty renamed the capital Zhongdu (Central Capital), and built an imperial palace in the city. Then they dredged and expanded the lake into a large reservoir, and heaped up ooze on the islet. Rocks

1 琼华岛上的白塔
White Pagoda on the Qionghuadao

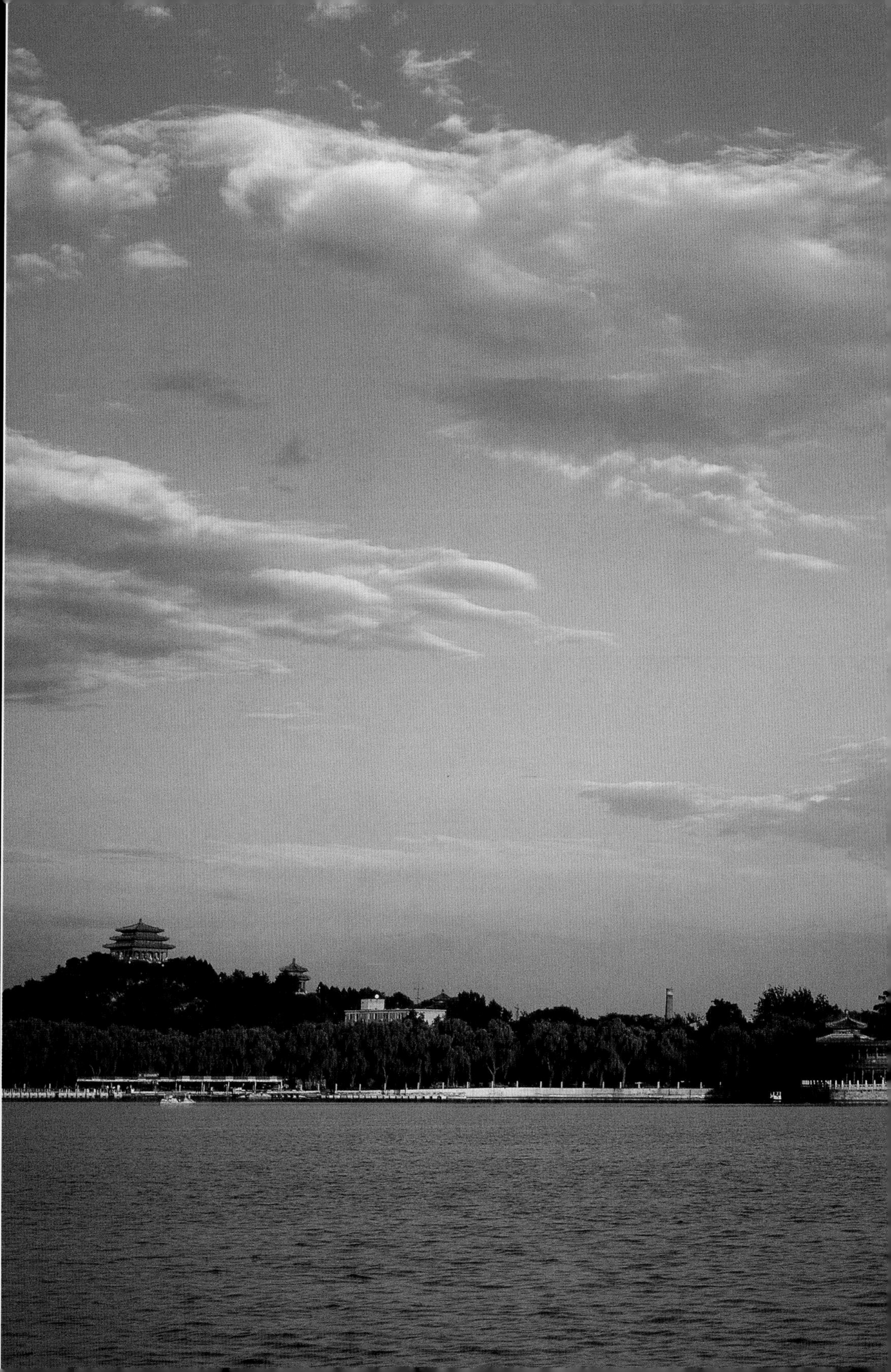

皇家宫苑·北海

44

used for piling on the hill were brought from Bianliang (today's Kaifeng).The islet was renamed Qionghuadao, on which Yao-guangdian (Palace of Jade Bright) and Guanghandian (Palace in the Moon) were added. The Beihai Park began to take shape. During the Yuan Dynasty, Kublai Khan planned his capital, the Yuan Dadu (Great Capital), centered by the Qionghuadao. The islet and lake were included in the imperial city and bestowed the new names, Wanshoushan (Longevity Hill) and Taiyechi (Celestial Pool). Thereafter, it was converted into a forbidden imperial garden in downtown, and is still situated in the heart of today's Beijing. In 1420, under Emperor Yongle's reign, the Ming court officially moved capital from Nanjing to Beijing. After the construction of the Forbidden City, the area became the Western Imperial Garden of the Ming emperors. The lake was extended to the south and divided into three lakes; various buildings were

constructed that remain today. Then Qing Dynasty saw more construction, and large-scale renovation and extension were carried out. During Shunzhi's reign, the white Dagoba in Tibetan style and Yong'ansi (Temple of Everlasting Peace) were built on the site of Guang-handian, and Wanshoushan was renamed Baitashan (Hill of White Dagoba). It is noteworthy that during the reign of Emperor Qianlong, construction lasted for 30 years, thus shaping present famous imperial garden.

The Beihai Park is an artistic masterpiece of China's classical garden. It has not only inherited China's tradition on building gardens in the past dynasties, but also widely absorbed the advanta-ges of garden building techniques in all regions. The park was exactly built according to Chinese ancient mythology, which says that in the ocean there were three celestial mountains, where celestial beings all lived in gorgeous pavilions and were in

the possession of pills of immortality. Rulers took to cons-tructing "celestial mountains" on the water space just outside the royal palace, turning legend into reality. The lake itself is remini-scent of the ocean, and Qiong-huadao, Tuancheng (Circular City) and Xishantai (Terrace of Xi Hill) symbolize the three celestial hills respectively. All the structures are laid out with the White Dagoba on the Qionghuadao as the center. In the south of the Dagoba a group of structures form a south-north axial line which extends to the Tuancheng, via the Yong'an (Eternal Peace) Bridge. Tens of structures were all built around the line. The eastern and northern banks of the lake are clustered with buildings as well. Tucked away in the woods or positioned abreast at the waterfront, they show great harmony of man and nature and extremely display the essence of art of Chinese classical gardening, looking like being made by nature.

团城位于北海南岸，城高4.6米，周长276米，面积约4500米。此处原是太液池中的一个小岛，金代为大宁宫一部分，元代称圆坻，亦称瀛洲。明永乐十五年（1417年）重修，改名承光殿。岛四周砌圆形城墙。清代重修扩建，成此规模。

On the southern shore of Beihai Lake lies an exquisitely built "city of cities". The miniature city in Beijing, the Tuancheng (Circular City) is 276 meters in circumference and 4,500 square meters in area. Surrounded by a 4.6-meter-high wall, it has a distinctive courtyard studded with halls, pavilions and ancient trees. It was originally an islet piled with ooze, which was a part of Daninggong (Palace of Grand Tranquility) built by the Liao rulers. A Yingzhou Round Hall was built on it during the Yuan Dynasty. Ming Emperor Yongle had it rebuilt and renamed it Chengguangdian (Hall of Receiving Light) in 1417, the 15th year of his reign, a round city wall was constructed as well. It was in the Qing Dynasty that the city was expanded as what we see today.

1　团城
　　Tuancheng

2　承光殿内玉佛
　　Jade Buddha in Chengguangdian

3　承光殿
　　Chengguangdian

承光殿是团城中的主体建筑，大殿坐北朝南，正方形，双重檐，黄琉璃瓦、绿剪边，四面有抱厦，其建筑形式颇似故宫角楼。承光殿内供有一尊释迦牟尼佛像，高1.5米，由整块纯正的白玉雕琢而成。全身洁白光润，袈裟及顶冠上镶以红绿宝石，光彩夺目。玉佛左臂上有一处刀痕，是八国联军入侵北京、抢掠宝石时所砍伤。院内玉瓮亭中有元代遗物大玉瓮——"渎山大玉海"，据说是元世祖忽必烈大宴群臣时盛酒的容器。

The Chengguangdian (Hall of Receiving Light), main structure in Tuancheng, is square in shape with porches on four sides. Facing south, the hall has a square platform in front and a double-eaved roof, which is covered with yellow glazed tiles and edged with green glazed tiles. It was rebuilt after the architectural style of the corner tower in the Forbidden City. In the hall is a 1.5-meter-high statue of Buddha of Sakyamuni, carved out of a very fine whole piece of white jade. The crown and kasaya are of gold foil and inlaid with red and green crystals. The knife scar on its left arm was made by the Eight-Power Allied Forces in 1900. Housed in the Yuwengting (Jade Urn Pavilion) in front of Chengguangdian is a big jade urn, which was believed to be a wine vessel of Kublai Khan, known as Dushandayuhai (Vast Jade-Sea of Du Hill).

45

皇家宫苑 · 北海

白塔位于琼华岛之巅，是北海四面风景的构图中心，也是北京的标志性建筑。白塔始建于清顺治八年（1651年），高35.9米，塔内有一根高30米的通天柱。塔底部为方形台基，上建三层圆台，承起圆塔肚。塔顶有铜制伞盖和镏金火焰宝珠的塔刹，使塔的形象更加鲜明突出。白色的塔身与蓝天、碧波、绿树构成一幅美丽的图画。

Standing high on the top of Qionghua-dao, the inverted-bowl-style Lamaist dagoba is the center of the surrounding scenery, and famous landmark in Beijing as well. Originally built in 1651, the 8th year of Qing Emperor Shunzhi's reign, the dagoba stands 35.9 meters high. It was built on a square stone base, and is topped by a copper canopy and a gilt flaming pearl. A 30-meter-tall pillar is erected inside it. Looked beautiful and majestic, the white body of the dagoba presents a sharp contrast with the blue sky, limpid waves as well as green woods.

1 *绿树掩映中的白塔*
  White Dagoba Cocooned in Green Woods

2 *白塔雪景*
  White Dagoba after Snow

著名的燕京八景之一"琼岛春阴"石碑位于白塔东北侧,这里建筑不多,但春景秀丽,树木成阴,苍翠欲滴。琼岛春阴碑碑首雕四龙戏珠,碑座为雕龙须弥座,碑高约4米。碑阳刻有乾隆亲笔书写的"琼岛春阴"四字,碑阴刻有他题写的御诗。

There is a famous "Qiongdao Chunyin (Jade Islet in Shady Spring-time) Stele" in the east side of the Qionghua Island, which was one of the "Eight Great Views of Yanjing". Amid the greenness, the 4-meter-high stele was erected on a stone Sumeru base carved with dragon motifs. Qing Emperor Qianlong once wrote a poem on it and inscribed four Chinese characters "Qiongdao Chunyin". The inscription was later carved on the facade of the tablet and the poem on the back.

3 夏日的北海
Beihai Park in Summer

4 "琼岛春阴"碑
Qiongdao Chunyin Sele

皇家宫苑 · 北海

47

静心斋，原名镜清斋，位于北海北岸，传说乾隆皇帝在此读过书，所以又名"乾隆小花园"；此处后来成为皇太子的书斋。静心斋是古代小园林中的精品，四周花墙依山势而建，园内布局精巧，风格独特。散布其间的楼、堂、亭、榭，或由水相隔，或由桥相连，回廊起伏，山石跌落，组成了多层次的景观。清光绪年间，在这里铺设了由中南海到北海沿湖岸的铁轨，此后每逢夏季慈禧太后都要乘小火车来静心斋避暑。

Jingxinzhai (Tranquil Heart Studio) on the northern shore of the Beihai Lake is an elaborately built garden of gardens. Originally called Jingqingzhai (Clear Mirror Study), it was where Emperor Qianlong read, so it was also known as the "Miniature Garden of Qianlong". Later, it was used as the study of the crown prince. Jingxinzhai is an exquisite example of classical Chinese gardens. Surrounded by a painted zigzag wall that follows the shape of the hills, the whole garden is ingeniously designed and novel in style. Towers, chambers pavilions and water-houses studded in the garden are separated by water or linked with bridges; the corridor climbs up and down the hill; the shore of the pond is decorated with piled rocks — they together give a three-dimensional impression of scenes and sights. Cixi once had a special narrow-gauge railway built along the bank of the Beihai Lake, which stretched from her residence at Zhongnanhai to entrance of the garden. Every summer, she came here to escape from the summer heat.

北海北岸西部临水建有五座亭子，合称五龙亭，亭间有石桥相连，是北海北岸最著名的景点。中央的龙泽亭体量最大，双重檐，上圆下方，突入水中，是清代皇帝钓鱼、赏月、观看焰火的游乐之处。

The Five Dragon Pavilions, connected by zigzag stone bridges at the waterfront, are a major scene on the northern shore of the Beihai Lake. Longzeting (Pavilion of the Dragon's Benevolence) in the middle stretches into the water and is the largest. Having double eaves — the up-

per is round while the lower square — this pavilion was where Qing emperors and their royal family went fish, admire the moon and watched fireworks.

1 **静心斋内的水榭**
   Water-house in Jingxinzhai

2 **静心斋**
   A View of Jingxinzhai

3 **静心斋内长廊**
   Covered Corridor in Jingxinzhai

4 **航拍琼华岛**
   An Aerial Photograph of Qionghuadao

5 **俯瞰五龙亭**
   A Bird's Eye View of Five Dragon Pavilions

6 **承露盘**
   Bronze Dew Plate

　　北海的九龙壁位于北海北岸天王殿之西，是中国现有三座九龙壁中最壮美的一处皇家龙壁。它高6.65米，厚1.2米，总长27米，全部由琉璃瓦砌筑。在五彩琉璃砌成的九龙壁两面，各有九条巨龙戏珠于翻腾的云海之中，姿态各异，造型活泼。九龙壁的装饰无处不雕龙，从正脊到盖筒瓦，大大小小共有600余条，堪称中国古代琉璃建筑中的精品。

West of the Tianwangdian (Hall of Heavenly Kings) on the northern shore of the Beihai Lake stands the Nine-Dragon Screen, the most beautiful of the three Nine-Dragon Screens extant in China. The screen wall is 6.65 meters high, 27 meters long and 1.2 meters thick, and was covered entirely with glazed color bricks. On either side of the wall is embedded with nine dragons in gay color and lively images. In different postures the dragons equally portray fierceness and vigor, tumbling in midst of clouds and waves. Additionally, the front ridges, fallen ridges and the tube-shaped tile heads are decorated with more than 600 dragons. The Nine-Dragon Screen has been the most precious works among the craft constructions by the colored glaze in China.

1 九龙壁局部
Glazed Dragons

2 九龙壁
Nine-Dragon Screen

天坛
Temple of Heaven

天坛，坐落于北京城区东南部，为明、清两代帝王祭天、祈谷的场所，是世界现存规模最大的祭天建筑群。天坛始建于明永乐十八年（1420年），与紫禁城同时兴建。经过历代，尤其是清乾隆年间修葺，形成今日规模。明、清两朝共有22个皇帝在此举行过600多次祭天大典。1914年，窃国大盗袁世凯在天坛举行了最后一次祭天活动。

天坛占地273万平方米，自成一条中轴线建筑体系。其建筑所独具的象征性布局和设计，奇特巧妙，处处体现着古人"天人合一"思想，是建筑和景观完美结合的杰作，朴素而鲜明地体现出中华文化中主要的宇宙观。天坛南端围墙呈方形，北端围墙是半圆形，象征古代"天圆地方"的天地观。天坛整个建筑布局呈"回"字形，由两道坛墙围成内外两坛，主体建筑均位于内坛之中，坐落在中轴线之上。内坛北部以祈年殿为中心的一组建筑群是祈谷坛，皇帝在这里举行祈谷大典，祈求丰年；南部以圜丘台、皇穹宇为主的建筑群是圜丘坛，皇帝在这里举行祭天大典。一条长360米的海墁大道纵贯南北，将两坛连成一个有机的整体。除此之外，天坛还有两组与众不同的建筑群，即斋宫和神乐署。斋宫实际是座小皇宫，是皇帝举行祭祀期间居住和斋戒的地方。神乐署则是专门负责祭祀时礼乐演奏的一个常设机构。天坛还建有宰牲亭、神厨、神库、牺牲所等附属建筑，是一组完整、典型的礼制建筑群。

园内遍植松柏，古木参天，肃穆静谧，环境幽雅，与庄严神秘的祭坛一起营造出一种古朴典雅、祥和宁静的氛围，使天坛更具魅力。

天坛集中国古代政治、哲学、天文、历法、音乐、绘画、园林，特别是建筑艺术、技术之精华于一身，具有深厚而广博的文化内涵，不仅是中国建筑史上罕见的杰作，也是世界现存古建筑的珍贵遗产。1998年12月，联合国教科文组织将其作为文化遗产项目列入《世界遗产名录》。

Located in the southeast of Beijing, the Temple of Heaven was where the emperors of Ming and Qing dynasties worshipped the heaven and prayed for good harvests. It is the largest architectural complex in this world for rituals to pay homage to heaven. A total of 22 Ming and Qing emperors had held more than 600 ceremonies to worship the Heaven here. One of the latest events of heaven worship was held in 1915 by Yuan Shikai.

1 航拍圜丘坛和皇穹宇
A Panorama View of Yuanqiutan and Huangqiongyu

皇家宫苑·天坛

Covering an area of 273 hectares, the Temple of Heaven forms an architectural system with its own axial line. The unique design and symbolic layout of the Temple have embodied ancient Chinese thought of "complete harmony of man and nature". It has been recognized as a masterpiece combining architecture with scenery seamlessly, as well as a distinct and simple demonstration of cosmos outlook in Chinese traditional culture. To better symbolize heaven and earth, the northern part of the Temple is circular while the southern part is square, which reflect the ancient Chinese belief that Heaven is round and Earth is square. The temple is divided by two enclosed walls into inner altar and outer altar. The main buildings of the temple lie at the south and north ends of the central axis line of the inner altar. Located in the northern part of the temple is the complex of Qigutan (Altar of Prayer for Grain), where the emperors sacrificed animals and burned incense sticks to pray for good weather for the crops; while in the southern part is the complex of Yuanqiutan (Circular Mound Altar) where emperors held ceremonies for worshipping the Heaven. Two principle clusters of worshipping buildings are connected by the Danbiqiao (Red Stairway Bridge). Additionally, in the temple are Zhaigong (Hall of Abstinence) where emperors held fasts before the ceremony and Shenyueshu (Divine Music Hall), an imperial organization in charge of performing during the ceremonies. There are also such subsidiary buildings as the Zai-shengting (Sacrifice-Butchering Pavilion), Shenchu (Divine Kitchen), Shenku (Divine Warehouse) and Xishengsuo (Sacrifice House), making it an integrated and typical ritual architectural compound. Many cypress and pine trees were planted during the Ming and Qing in the Temple, which create an atmosphere of grandeur and quietness.

The Temple of Heaven is a crystallization of the politics, philosophy, astronomy, calen-dar, music, painting and garden constructing of ancient China, as well as architectural skill and technology. Not only is the Temple of Heaven a scarce masterwork in the history of Chinese architecture, but also a precious heritage of world existing ancient architecture. In 1998, it was inscribed on the World Heritage List by the UNESCO.

1 气势恢宏的祈年殿
   Imposing Qiniandian
2 祈谷坛雪景
   Snow Scenery of Qigutan

1

祈年殿是祈谷坛的主体建筑，为明、清帝王举行祈谷大典的地方。祈年殿坐落在高约5.2米的三层汉白玉圆台之上，四面环以栏板及望柱，正面中陛每层雕有一帧巨大的汉白玉浮雕，上、中、下三层浮雕的主题分别是双龙山海、双凤山海和瑞云山海，各层石栏的望柱头和出水嘴的形象也相应为龙、凤、云。大殿通高32米，坐落在三层汉白玉圆台之上，为三重檐圆攒尖顶式建筑。三重檐均覆以蓝色琉璃瓦，鎏金宝顶，玉立苍穹。

祈年殿是一座无与伦比的建筑。大殿由28根楠木大柱支撑，不用一根铁钉，仅凭木榫穿插、斗拱支架，使整个建筑成为一个完整、结实的架构系统，堪称中国木结构建筑中的精品。

祈年殿是每年农历正月上辛日举行祈谷大典的场所。清朝大典时，殿内雕龙宝座上供奉满汉合璧的"皇天上帝"神版，

东西两侧设有配位，供奉的是清朝历代皇帝，以体现古人"敬天法祖"的意识。每个神位前都设有供桌，陈放各种供品。

28根大柱分三环排列，内环四根高19.2米，直径1.2米，代表着一年春、夏、秋、冬四个季节；中环12根金柱，象征着一年十二个月；外环12根檐柱，象征一日12个时辰。外环、中环24根柱子代表二十四节气；全部28根大柱代表二十八星宿，再加上柱顶的八根雷公柱，象征三十六天罡星。从某种意义上说，祈年殿是一座时间建筑。它充分反映了中国古代对于天文历法的精确计算和研究水平，也体现了古人"重农"的思想。

祈年殿殿内满饰龙凤和玺彩画，金碧辉煌，28根大柱支撑着三重屋檐，殿顶层层收缩，叠落起来形成穹隆，中为龙凤藻井，金龙飞舞，彩凤翩翩，高贵华美，富丽堂皇。

The Qiniandian (Hall of Prayer for Good Harvests), core structure of the Qigutan (Altar of Prayer for Grain) was where the Ming and Qing emperors held ceremonies for good harvests. First built in 1420, the hall stands on a round 5.2-meter-high white marble base, which comprises three tiers. Each tier is surrounded by white marble railing boards and balustrades. There is a huge white marble stairway on the middle of stair of each tier, with the relief of patterns of clouds, phoenix and dragon respectively, from bottom to top. Correspondingly, the railing boards, balustrades and drainage outlets of each tire are carved the same patterns. The Qiniandian, 32 meters in height, is a lofty cone-shaped structure with triple eaves, covered by blue glazed tiles, and the top is crowned by a gilded ball. This majestic hall looks as if it was a colossus that might prop up the sky from the ground.

No beams, no crossbeams, no nails, the vault of Qiniandian is solely supported by 28 massive wooden pillars and a number of bars, lathes, joints and rafters, which are integrated into a reinforced frame to keep up the bulk of the hall. This hall is an outstanding structure of all Chinese wooden buildings.

The Qiniandian was the place where ceremonies of praying for good harvests were held in the first month of spring. In the center of the hall is a throne with carvings of dragon-pattern, placed on which is the tablet of heaven, bearing the inscription "the Emperor of Heaven" both in Manchu and Chinese languages. Also enthroned in the hall are tablets of deceased emperors of the Qing Dynasty, which shows the emperor's respect to the Heaven and his ancestors. Many items were placed in front of each shrine as the offerings.

In the Qiniandian, 28 pillars were arranged in three rings. The four central pillars are 19.2 meters high and 1.2 meters in diameter, and painted with designs of composite flowers, representing the four seasons. The 12 gilded pillars in the middle ring represent 12 months; the outer 12 pillars represent 12 hours of a

day (by way of Chinese ancient time-reckoning). 12 gilded pillars and 12 outer pillars together represent 24 solar terms of a year; all 28 huge pillars represent 28 constellations in the universe; and these 28 huge pillars and the 8 small pillars setting above the four central pillars together represent the 36 stars in the space. The arrangement of pillars reflects Chinese people's knowing about "the Heaven" in ancient time, and their paying attention to the agriculture. It is indeed a building of time.

All the beams and lintels of the Qiniandian are painted with patterns of dragon and phoenix and colorful imperial paintings, looks splendid and elegant. The 28 huge pillars support three layers of ceilings, which lead to the top dragon-phoenix caisson. The patterns of dragon and phoenix are absolutely lifelike.

1 祈年殿内景
   Interior of Qiniandian
2 俯瞰祈年殿
   A Bird's Eye View of Qiniandian
3 龙凤藻井
   Dragon-Phoenix Caisson

圜丘台又叫祭天台，为明、清皇帝举行祭天大典的场所。圜丘台始建于明嘉靖九年（1530年），当时规模较小，台面以青色琉璃砖铺墁，周围的栏板及柱子皆为青色琉璃。清乾隆十四年（1749年）扩建将台面改为艾叶青石，栏板及柱子全用汉白玉，一直保留至今。

圜丘台是中国古代石材建筑的代表之作。台共分三层，通高5.17米。上层直径23米多，中心为一块圆石，名"天心石"。坛面围绕"天心石"以扇面形状向外展开上层第一重有九块石板，其余各重石块数均为九的倍数。建造者巧妙地运用了数学知识，将建筑物与数字完美地结合起来充分体现了古人"天人合一"的思想，展示了中国古代劳动人民的智慧和想象。

圜丘台有两道围墙，外墙为方形，每边长约168米；内墙为圆形，直径约10米，体现了古人"天圆地方"的学说。两道墙共设24座棂星门，汉白玉雕成。但每组棂星门大小不一。大典时，中间最高大的为"天帝"专用，右侧较窄的供皇帝出入，陪祭的大臣只能从最窄的门通过。

Also known as Jitiantai (Heaven-Worshipping Terrace), the Yuanqiuta (Circular Mound) is the principal structure of the Yuanqiutan (Circular Mound Altar)

where the emperors offered sacrifice to Heaven on the day of the Winter Solstice every year. The three-tiered stone terrace was initially built in 1530, the ninth year of Ming Emperor Jiajing's reign period, and smaller in scale. It was originally surfaced with blue glazed bricks, and the railing boards and balustrades were made of blue glazed materials. In 1749, by the order of Qing Emperor Qianlong, it was expanded. The blue glazed bricks were changed into blue stones, and the railing boards and balustrades were made of white marble. Till today, the structure still stands perfectly, keeping the former appearance in Qianlong's reign.

The Yuanqiutai is a representative of ancient stone-made structures. 5.17 meters in height, it is a three-tiered stone terrace. The upper terrace is more than 23 meters in diameter, at the center of which lies a round stone surrounded by nine concentric rings of stones. The number of stones in the first ring is 9, in the second ring 18 and so on, up to the 81 in the ninth ring. The number of nine, as the largest positive number, was regarded as the symbol and the supremacy of the Heaven by ancients. Builders applied knowledge of mathematics, combined the structures and numbers finely, which was a complete harmony of man and nature, and crystallization of the wisdom and imagination of Chinese people in ancient times.

The Yuanqiutai is surrounded by two

walls, the inner wall, 102 meters in diameter, taking a round shape to resemble heaven while the outer one squared, 168 meters in length, to symbolize earth. Each wall contains four groups of Lingxing Gate, each of which consists of three doors, thus, there are totally 24 Lingxing Gates. The gates of each group are not same in size. The widest one in the middle was used exclusively by the Emperor of Heaven during the ceremonies, while the right one for the emperor, and ministers could

pass through the left gate, the narrowest one.

1 圜丘坛
  Yuanqiutan

2 天心石
  Heavenly Heart Stone

3 圜丘坛全景
  A Panorama View of Yuanqiutan

4 棂星门
  Lingxing Gate

5 汉白玉栏杆及栏板
  Marble Railing Boards and Balustrades

皇穹宇为圆形单檐攒尖顶建筑,鎏金宝顶,上覆蓝色琉璃瓦。大殿通高 19.5米,直径15.6米,坐落在2.85米高的圆形青白石须弥座上。该殿是在圜丘坛举行祭天大典后,存放皇天上帝神牌和清朝皇帝祖先神牌的地方。

皇穹宇正殿大木架构,由八根檐柱和八根金柱共同支撑。柱上无横梁,设鎏金斗拱,层层收缩,承托一圆形天花藻井,中心绘"大金团龙"。殿内满饰龙凤和玺彩画,庄重华贵,金碧辉煌。正殿前石阶正中,镶嵌一块巨大浮雕,上刻"双龙戏珠"图案。双龙一左一右,一升一降,雕工精美,栩栩如生。

皇穹宇的周围是一道灰墙体、蓝瓦檐的圆形围墙,即是皇穹宇最为奇妙的部分——回音壁。围墙高3.27米,长193.2米,磨砖对缝砌成,墙面坚硬光滑,是声波良好的反射体。一人站在围墙边小声说话,站在另一边的人可以清晰地听到,因此得名。

皇穹宇殿前东、西各有配殿一座,灰墙蓝瓦,歇山顶式,是祭天大典后存放祭祀牌位的地方。殿内供有日、月、星、辰、风、雷、雨、云等神灵的牌位。

The Huangqiongyu is a circular structure with a single-eaved pyramid roof which is covered with blue glazed tiles and topped by a gilded ball. Standing on a 2.85-meter-high round marble terrace, it is 19.5 meters in height and 15.6 meters in diameter. It was used to house the tablets of the God of Heaven and emperor's ancestors after the heaven worshipping ceremonies.

The whole structure is supported by 16 pillars on two rings, eight of which are posts propping the eaves and another eight inside are gilded one. On top of the pillars there are gilded bracket sets that support the ceiling. The dome is so constructed as to taper little by little and result in a vault, which is characterized by a golden coiling dragon design. In front of the Huangqiongyu, there is a huge stairway on the middle flight with the relief of "two dragons playing with one ball". Two dragons, the rising one on right and the falling one on left, are designed exquisite and carved elaborately.

Enclosing the Huangqiongyu is a grey wall covered with blue glazed tiles, which are 3.27 meters high and 193.2 meters long. It is the most wonderful part of the complex and known as the Echo Wall. Constructed with smooth and solid bricks, the wall enables a whisper to travel clearly from one end to the other, hence the name. This indicates that Chinese people had known how to apply the acoustic theory into buildings at the time.

Flanking Huangqiongyu are eastern and western secondary halls. Covered by blue tiles, these two halls have gray walls and beams resting on the gables. Tablets of Matching Gods, such as God of the Sun, Moon, Stars, Wind, Thunder, Rain, Clouds, and so on, were enshrined here after worshipping ceremonies.

1 皇穹宇内景
  Interior of Huangqiongyu
2 皇穹宇
  Huangqiongyu
3 皇穹宇殿前的丹陛
  Stairway in front of Huangqiongyu

皇
家
宫
苑
·
天
坛

丹陛桥是连接天坛南北两大主体建筑的轴线，为内坛的主轴线。全长360米，宽约30米，从南向北，逐渐升高，表示从人间到天上有遥远的路程。丹陛桥北端东侧建有具服台，台南北宽13.60米，东西长10.85米，北、东、南三面围以汉白玉石栏。举行祭天大典前，在具服台上搭建一方形黄缎子幄帐，皇帝在这里更换服饰，等待祭典时刻的来临。

The Danbiqiao connects the two groups of main buildings in the Temple of Heaven and constitutes a single axis. It is 360 meters long and 30 meters wide, and from south to north, it is gaining height gradually. Walking along the road, one could have a feeling, by degree, coming to the Heaven. Built on east side at the northern end of Danbiqiao is the Jufutai (Platform of Changing Clothes). It is 13.60 meters wide from south to north and 10.85 meters long from east to west, and surrounded by white marble balustrades in the north, east and south sides. The platform used to be the place where the emperor had a short rest to change clothes before starting the worshipping ceremonies.

1 回音壁
 Echo Wall
2 丹陛桥
 Danbiqiao

斋宫，又称"小皇宫"，是祭天大典前皇帝斋戒、休息的地方。斋宫为一座封闭的城池，布局严谨，环境典雅，四周围与两重围墙和两道御沟。内沟为U字形，东、南、北三面架设石桥。当年内外御沟里都注满水，形成了戒备森严的防御体系。

斋宫内建有正殿、寝宫、钟楼、值守房等，主体建筑均坐西朝东，覆以绿色琉璃瓦。表现了"皇天上帝"至高于上的地

位，以及作为"天子"的皇帝对天称臣，虔诚敬天。

斋宫正殿建于明永乐十八年（1420年），汉白玉殿基，庑殿顶，为砖券结构，整个殿堂无梁枋大木，故又称"无梁殿"。大殿分五间，是皇帝在斋戒期间召见大臣，处理政务的地方。殿前置放有斋戒铜人亭和时辰亭。前者为警示皇帝恪守戒律、诚心斋戒之用，后者是皇帝祭天时供奉时辰牌位的地方。

The Zhaigong (Palace of Abstinence), also called "Lesser Imperial Palace", was where the emperor prepared himself in abstinence before he offered sacrifices at important ceremonies. It is a closed city, surrounded by double enclosing walls and two moats, known as the Im-

3 斋宫正门
Front Gate of Zhaigong

penal Ditch. The inner moat is in shape
of "U" character. There were stone
bridges spanning across the moats on the
three sides of east, south and north. As
the defensive structure, the moats were
filled with water in the past.

The main buildings in Zhaigong are the
main hall, rest hall, bell tower, watch
house, and so on. All of them face east
and are covered with green glazed tiles
showing the supreme statue of the heavenly god and emperor's greatest respect
to him.

Constructed in 1420, the main Hall of
Zhaigong is situated on a terrace made
of white marble. The hall is made of brick
and has a hip roof. The entire building
has none wooden beam or pillar, so it is
also known as the Beamless Hall. Consisting of five rooms, the hall was the
place emperors summoned ministers and

conducted state affairs during the fasting time. Placed in front of the hall are two stone pavilions. The left one housed a bronze figurine, which was used to warn the emperors not to forget the regulations of fasting; while the right housed tablet of the time to mark the time of the worshipping ceremony. The time of ceremony was about 4 o'clock in the morning.

1 御沟
   Imperial Ditch
2 斋宫全景
   Full View of Zhaigong
3 无梁殿
   Beamless Hall
4 寝宫
   Rest Palace
5 斋宫内门
   Inner Gate of Zhaigong

3

4

5

皇家宫苑 · 天坛

皇家宫苑·天坛

4

5

1 **古柏**
Ancient Cypress

2 **古柏和长廊**
Ancient Cypress and Corridor

3 **九龙柏**
Nine-Dragon Cypress

4 **双环万寿亭和扇面亭**
Shuanghuan Wanshou (Double-Ring Longevity) Pavilion and Shanmian (Fan-Shaped) Pavilion

5 **扇面亭**
Shanmian Pavilion

6 **俯瞰天坛中轴线**
Full View of the Architectural Structures on the Central Axis of the Temple of Heaven

6

颐和园
Summer Palace

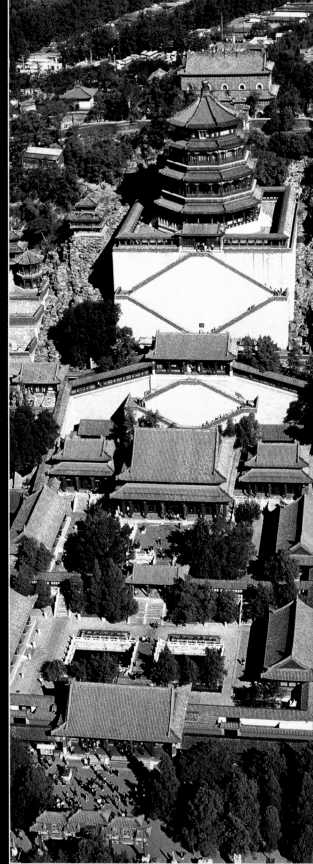

颐和园位于北京市西北郊,是中国著名的古典皇家园林,总面积达290多万平方米,主要由万寿山和昆明湖组成。

颐和园的前身为金代行宫。后来,元世祖忽必烈命都水监郭守敬将水域疏浚扩展成为北京西郊的大水库;并把湖中挖出的土堆砌于山之上。明弘治七年(1494年),孝宗皇帝在此修建了圆静寺。其后,酷爱游山玩水的明武宗朱厚照修建好山园行宫。

18世纪中叶,中国古典园林的建筑经过了历朝各代的造园实践,继承并综合各代艺术成就,水平达到顶峰,形成了完整的艺术体系,皇家园林的兴建也已进入鼎盛时期。清乾隆十五年(1750年),乾隆皇帝在此大兴土木,修建清漪园,前后用时15年。完工后的清漪园不仅继承了中国北方园林的恢宏大气,又兼具江南园林的秀美多姿,更将京城西北郊的皇家园林连接成片,构成一组完整的园林体系。清咸丰十年(1860年),英法联军攻入北京,清漪园内木结构建筑均被付之一炬。光绪十一年(1885年),垂帘听政的慈禧太后,挪用海军经费开始动工修复清漪园,并将其改名为颐和园。1900年,颐和园再次遭到八国联军的破坏和洗劫。后因清廷没落,慈禧只是对前山和园内东部进行了再次修缮。1924年,颐和园被辟为公园。新中国成立后,政府多次拨款修葺,再现了这座皇家园林辉煌的景观布局。1998年,颐和园被联合国教科文组织作为文化遗产项目列入《世界遗产名录》。

颐和园是北京现存规模最大,保存最完整的清代园林。园内集中了中国古典建筑的精华,容纳了不同地区的园林风格,堪称园林建筑博物馆。昆明湖水域辽阔,约占全园面积的四分之三。湖区西部由一条长堤和一条短堤将昆明湖分割为三部分,每片水域建有一座小岛,构成了"一池三山"的仙国境界,体现出帝王追求长生不老的构园思想。由万寿山山脚至山顶,层层叠建了以佛香阁为主的重重高大雄伟的建筑,构成全园景观的中心。30多组古典建筑或散布湖边,或隐没山林,或金碧辉煌,或小巧可人,使游人顿生天上人间之感。颐和园不愧是中国园林艺术的瑰宝。

Situated in the northwest suburb of Beijing, the Summer Palace is a famous classical imperial garden, which covers an area of 290 hectares and comprises mainly the Wanshoushan (Longevity Hill) and Kunming Lake.

The predecessor of the Summer Palace was a provisional palace of the Jin Dynasty. During the Yuan

1 佛香阁建筑群
Foxiangge Complex

皇家宫苑·颐和园

Dynasty, Kublai Khan had Guo Shoujing dredged and expanded the lake into a large reservoir, and heaped up ooze on the hill. In 1494, Ming Emperor Xiaozong built the Yuanjingsi (Temple of Perfection and Tranquility) here. Then, Emperor Wuzong of the same dynasty built the Haoshanyuan (Garden of Marvelous Hill) on the site.

By the mid-18th century, the architecture of Chinese classical gardens had inherited and synthesized artistic achievements of past dynasties, and reached an unprecedented high peak. Construction of imperial gardens entered its heyday. In 1750, or the 15th year of the Qianlong Reign of the Qing Dynasty, Emperor Qianlong went on a construction and renamed the place Qingyiyuan (Garden of Rippling Ripples). Construction of the garden lasted for 15 years. Architecturally, the garden blends the style of the lower Yangtze valley with the architectural pattern of the north. It also linked up the imperial gardens in the northwestern suburbs of Beijing to form a complete garden system, known as the "Three

Hills and Five Gardens". In 1860, the Anglo-French Allied Force burned it to the ground. All wooden structures in Qingyiyuan were burnt to ashes. Later, in 1885, Cixi embezzled funds from the Imperial Navy and restored the garden. In 1888 when the project was about to be completed, Cixi renamed it Yiheyuan (literally, the Garden of Health and Peace), or the Summer Palace, as it is known to foreigners today. However, in 1900, the Summer Palace was ravaged once more by the Eight-Power Allied Forces. The invaders took away everything valuable and destroyed the buildings. The Qing court was, by this time, reduced to such financial shortage that it was unable to allocate any money for restoration, so only the front of Longevity Hill and the eastern part of the garden had been rebuilt. In 1924, the Summer Palace was opened to the public as a park. The garden was reborn after the founding of the People's Republic of China in 1949. The government of New China has been funding to renovate most ramshackle buildings and scenic

spots according to their original designs and to reappear their former grandeur. In 1998, the UNESCO inscribed the Summer Palace on the World Heritage List.

The largest and best-preserved imperial garden of the Qing Dynasty extant in Beijing, the Summer Palace is a veritable museum of garden-type architecture of different styles from different regions in China, and is definitely a gem in the Chinese art of garden construction. Natural scenery is skillfully combined with man-made scenes and sights to form a garden of breathtaking beauty. The charm of Kunming Lake lies in the vast expanse of water, which covers nearly three-fourths of the area of the Summer Palace. Long and short dykes have been built to divide the Kunming Lake in three parts, and three isles were constructed to symbolize the celestial hills in ancient mythology and give expression to the emperors' desire for immortality. The entire slope of the Longevity Hill is covered by several groups of giant buildings, with the Foxiangge in the center. More than 30 classical structures are scattered on the hill and around the lake. The rich verdure of the hill, the rippling water in the lake, the golden glory of the pavilions and halls, combine to engender the feeling in the visitor that he was walking in heaven. The Summer Palace is definitely a gem in the Chinese art of garden construction and the world history of garden construction and horticulture.

1 东宫门
Eastern Palace Gate

颐和园按各部分功用可分为政治活动区、帝后生活区和风景游览区。仁寿殿是政治活动区的主要建筑。该殿始建于1750年，是园中最重要的政治活动场所。慈禧太后和光绪皇帝曾在此坐朝听政、接见外国使臣和他们的夫人。殿内按当年帝后临朝听政时陈设，中间设置宝座、御案、掌扇等；宝座后装饰有一座写有200多个不同字体的"寿"字屏风。仁寿殿前正中月台上，设有一尊青铜兽像，它名为麒麟，龙头、鹿角、狮尾、牛蹄，周身遍布鳞甲，是神话传说中的瑞兽，可以驱除邪恶。置于此象征国泰民安。

According to various functions, the Summer Palace is divided into three sections: administrative area, imperial residential area and scenic area. The Renshoudian (Hall of Benevolence and Longevity) was the core structure of the administrative area. Initially built in 1750, it was the most important hall for political activities in the garden. Empress Dowager Cixi and Emperor Guangxu handled state affairs and received foreign envoys and their wives here. The arrangement

of the hall has been left untouched. In the middle of the hall, there stands the emperor's throne and table. Two fans on each side of the throne represent the dignity of the emperor. Behind the throne is a red sandalwood screen, on which more than 200 Chinese characters meaning "longevity" were written in different scripts. There is a bronze *kylin* on a platform in front of the hall. Also known as unicorn, a *kylin* has the head of a dragon, the antlers of a deer, the tail of a lion and the hooves of an ox and is covered with a scaled-skin, which was considered an auspicious creature in myths that could drive out evil spirits. It was placed there to symbolize that the country was prosperous and the people were at peace.

2 东宫门匾额及丹陛
Horizontal Board and Stairway
3 仁寿殿
Renshoudian
4 仁寿殿内景
Interior of Renshoudian

74

乐寿堂是帝后生活区的主要建筑。整个建筑群为一组两进四合院，左右各带跨院，殿堂红墙灰瓦，歇山式顶，廊枋遍饰彩画，造型别致，环境清幽。光绪年间，慈禧太后将这里作为寝宫。乐寿堂阶前对称陈列着铜鹤、铜鹿和铜瓶，取"鹿、鹤、瓶"的谐音，喻意"六合太平"。

帝后生活区还有一座重要的建筑，即玉澜堂。玉澜堂是一座临湖而建的四合院式建筑。光绪实行"戊戌变法"失败后，被慈禧太后囚于中南海瀛台。玉澜堂为慈禧太后在颐和园内囚禁光绪皇帝的地方。

The Leshoutang (Hall of Happiness and Longevity) is the central structure of the imperial residential area, with quiet and tasteful layout and pleasant surroundings. The magnificent complex consists of a forecourt and a backyard with annex courts on each side. Main building has red walls, gray tiles and a gable-hip roof. The beams and lintels are decorated with colored-paintings. Flanking the steps leading to the main entrance of the hall, there are bronze cranes, deer and vases, symbolizing universal peace.

Another important building in this area is Yulantang (Hall of Jade Ripples). It is a group of special and quiet courtyard dwellings by water. In 1898, the Reform Movement was carried out by Guangxu's order. But Cixi suppressed the movement. From then on, he had been confined. It was in Yulantang that Guangxu was under house arrest when Cixi stayed in the Summer Palace.

1 乐寿堂内景
  Interior of Leshoutang
2 慈禧卧室
  Cixi's Bedroom
3 乐寿堂外景
  Leshoutang
4 玉澜堂内景
  Interior of Yulantang
5 扬仁风
  Yangrenfeng (Hall of Creating the Atmosphere of Benevolence)

皇家宫苑·颐和园

德和园占地3000多平方米，共分三进院落，主要由大戏楼、颐乐殿和庆善堂等组成，是一组专供帝后看戏用的建筑群。

德和园大戏楼是中国目前保存最完整、规模最大的古戏楼，与北京故宫的"畅音阁"、承德避暑山庄的"清音阁"并称"清宫三大戏楼"。戏楼通高21米，底部舞台宽17米，分为三层，可同时演出，戏台之间设有"天井"相通。大戏楼建成之后，慈禧太后经常让社会上的名演员进宫演出，当时许多著名的京剧表演艺术家，如谭鑫培、杨小楼等，都曾在此表演。

Covering an area of over 3,000 square meters, the Deheyuan (Garden of Virtu-

ous Harmony), where emperor and empress of the Qing Dynasty were entertained with Beijing Opera performances, mainly consists of Daxitai (Grand Theater), Yiledian (Hall of Health and Happiness), and Qingshantang (Hall in Celebration of Philanthropy).

The Grand Theater of the Deheyuan is the best preserved and largest ancient theater in existence in China today. It was one of the three major theaters of the Qing court along with the Changyinge (Pavilion of Cheerful Melodies) of the Forbidden City and the Qingyinge (Pavilion of the Tower of Clear Voice) of

the Mountain Resort of Cheng-de. The stage stands 21 meters tall and 17 meters wide. Featuring three floors linked with each other by air raises, the theater is known for its superb acoustic effect. The three floors are connected by trap-doors, which provide convenience for actors to appear and disappear. Since the completion of the Grand Theater, Empress Dowager Cixi often sent for famous actors to give performances on the stage. It played a major part in fostering the birth and development of Beijing Opera, and was known as the "Cradle of Beijing Opera". Many accomplished performers, such as Tan Xinpei and Yang Xiaolou, once played here.

1　大戏楼的戏台
　　Stage of Grand Theater

2　德和园大戏楼
　　Deheyuan Grand Theater

3　颐乐殿
　　Yiledian

4　慈禧宝座
　　Cixi's Throne

皇家宫苑 · 颐和园

佛香阁始建于乾隆十五年(1750年),后被英法联军烧毁,光绪十七年(1891年)重建而成。阁楼是一座三层四重檐八角攒式顶的宗教建筑,通高近40米,建于前山20米高的石砌台基之上,使它耸立在半山之上,气势尤为磅礴。

佛香阁结构独特,布局紧凑。各层屋顶均覆以黄色琉璃瓦,门窗、立柱等均为红色,在漫山绿树的衬托之下,形象十分突出,将万寿山一带的优美风景提携于周围,从而成为全园的造景中心。

佛香阁内一层供奉着"南无大悲观世音菩萨"。佛像铸造于明万历二年(1574年),高达5米,共有12张面孔、36只眼睛和24只手臂,立于雕刻有999个花瓣的莲花宝座之上,雕工细腻,技艺精湛。

The Foxiangge (Tower of Buddhist Incense) was first constructed in 1750, or the 15th year of Emperor Qianlong's reign, but destroyed by fire by Anglo-French troops, and then rebuilt in 1891. An octagonal structure under a four-eaved roof, it was a religious building. The imposing tower itself is about 40 meters tall, and elevated on a stone platform 20 meters in height, so that the entire tower stands in the middle of the hill slope.

The eaves of the various floors of this tower are fringed with yellow glazed tiles, and the pillars, doors and windows are painted crimson, so that the structure stands out strikingly in the midst of green trees. With its unique structure, ingenious layout, towering terrace and convincing grandeur, the Foxiangge was artfully set out by the imperial gardens and beautiful scenery surrounding it, making it the very center of the whole garden. It is one of the masterpieces of ancient Chinese architecture.

Enshrined in the Foxiangge is the statue of Avalokitesvara Bodhisattvais, who has 12 faces, 36 eyes and 24 arms, standing on a precious pedestal of 999 lotus petals. Five meters in height, the exquisite statue was cast in 1574, the second year of Ming Emperor Wanli's reign.

1 排云殿
  Paiyundian
2 佛香阁雄姿
  Foxiangge Standing on Platform
3 气势磅礴的佛香阁
  Towering Foxiangge
4 远眺佛香阁建筑群
  Viewing Foxiangge Complex from Afar

皇家宫苑·颐和园

铜亭，又叫宝云阁，是喇嘛为帝后祈祷念经的场所，建于1755年，重檐歇山顶，全部构件为仿木铜铸。亭高7.55米，重达207吨，坐落在汉白玉须弥座上，外形庄重，花纹精细，极为精美。

Built in 1755, the Bronze Pavilion, or the Baoyunge (Pavilion of Precious Clouds) was where lamas chanted scriptures and prayed for emperor and empress. The entire structure, having a double-eaved gable-hip roof, is 7.55 meters in height and 207 tons in weight. Sitting on a white marble base, the pavilion is made entirely of bronze, with exquisite decorative patterns on its walls and looks extremely elaborately. Unfortunately, the pavilion met with catastrophe twice in 1860 and 1900.

1　**佛香阁和昆明湖**
　Foxiangge and Kunming Lake
2　**佛香阁内的观音像**
　Statue Enshrined in Foxiangge
3　**铜亭局部**
　Carvings on the Bronze Pavilion
4　**铜亭**
　Bronze Pavilion
5　**石舫**
　Marble Boat

石舫，又名清晏舫，位于昆明湖北端西侧。它通长36米，船体全部用巨大石块雕凿而成，上建两层舱楼，雕梁画栋，精美无比。舱内花砖铺地，窗上镶嵌五彩玻璃，顶部以砖雕装饰。石舫始建于1755年，既是为了观赏昆明湖景色，又用以象征清王朝的统治如"磐石"般巩固。原石舫毁于1860年。1894年慈禧重修颐和园时，修建现在这座石舫，将舱楼改为洋式，并改名"清晏舫"，寓意"河清海晏"。

Off the northern shore of the lake is the Marble Boat, 36 meters in length. Built entirely of huge stone slabs, it is also known as Qingyanfang (Boat of Purity and Ease). The two-floor pavilion on the boat is decorated with carved beams and lacquered pillars. The ground was paved with floral bricks, all of the windows were inlaid with multi-colored glass, and the ceiling was decorated with carved bricks. The presence of this marble, which was first built in 1755, facilitated seeing and sights on the lake and symbolized the rock-firm of the Qing Dynasty. The original boat was destroyed in 1860 by the Anglo-French troops when they invaded Beijing. In 1894, Empress Dowager Cixi rebuilt it in Western style and renamed Qingyanfang, meaning universal peace.

皇家宫苑·颐和园

万寿山南坡的建筑因地构筑，设计巧妙。山屏于北，水拥于南，一条长廊沿岸而设，与佛香阁建筑群垂直相交，将颐和园内无限美好的湖光山色连接在一起。

长廊东起邀月门，西止石丈亭，全长728米，共273间。长廊以排云门为中心，左右对称，布局严谨，两侧建有四座重檐八角亭和两座水榭。四座亭子，自东而西依次为留佳、寄澜、秋水、清遥，象征一年四季。

长廊蜿蜒曲折，移步换景，每根梁枋上都绘有精美的苏式彩画，共计14000余幅，题材广泛，内容丰富，主要有花木虫鸟，人物故事，山水风景等。其中人物故事大多出自中国古典文学名著《红楼梦》、《西游记》《三国演义》《水浒》《封神演义》《聊斋》等。

The Summer Palace is marked by two lines that meet at right angles. A cluster of grand buildings ascending gradually from the water to the summit of the hill according to the terrain form the south-north line, and the east-west line is the famous Long Corridor. With a hill in the north while a lake in the south, the corridor stretches along the shore, and, like a floating ribbon, knits the various scenic spots into an integral whole.

The 273-section corridor begins at the Yaoyuemen (Gate for Inviting Moon) and runs for a total distance 728 meters through the Paiyunmen (Cloud-Dispelling Gate), four octagonal double-eaved pavilions and two waterside chambers, until it reaches the Shizhangting (Pavilion of Master Stone). Taking Pai-yunmen as the center, the corridor extends in both directions symmetrically. The four pavilions are Liujia (Beauty-Retaining), Jilan (Enjoy-the-Ripples), Qiushui (Autumn Water) and Qingyao (Clarity Distance) from east to west, symbolizing the four seasons.

The Long Corridor is a colorful gallery. Its eaves and beams are gaily painted with pictures covering a wide range of subjects of flowers, trees, worms, birds, human figures, and scenery, such as lotus flowers blooming on ponds, flying birds through forests, fish swimming in water. Some of the paintings tell about history and historical figures, most of which come from Chinese literary classics such as *A Dream of Red Mansions*, *Journey to the West*, *Romance of the Three Kingdom*, *Outlaws of the Marsh*, *Creation of the Gods*, *Strange Tales from Make-Do Studio*, and others.

1 邀月门
  Yaoyuemen
2 蜿蜒曲折的长廊
  Zigzag Long Corridor
3 孙悟空大闹天宫
  Colored Painting of Monkey King
4 一眼望不到尽头的长廊
  Endless Corridor

皇
家
宫
苑
·
颐
和
园

谐趣园位于颐和园东北角,建于乾隆年间,为仿江苏无锡寄畅园而修建的一座具有江南私家园林特色的园中之园。园中央为一水池,亭、台、堂、榭,环水坐落,百间游廊串联相通,建筑小巧,布局精致。每到夏季,荷花吐艳,花香扑鼻,俨然一派江南景色。

Situated in the northeast corner of the Summer Palace, the Xiequyuan, a garden within gardens, was built during Qianlong's reign and fashioned according to the design and layout of the Jichangyuan (Garden for Ease of Mind) in Wuxi, Jiangsu Province. Despite its limited space, the garden provided a kaleidoscopic view. A pond lies in the center of the garden, and on the shore are more than a dozen pavilions, chambers, halls, waterhouses as well as corridors and bridges, laid out in a picturesque manner to form a quiet environment reflecting the atmosphere of southern China garden.

1 谐趣园雪景
  Snowy Scene of Xiequyuan
2 夏日的谐趣园
  Xiequyuan in Summer
3 后山全景
  A Panoramic View of Rear Slopes
4 西堤航拍
  An Aerial Photograph of Xidi Dyke

1

皇家宫苑·颐和园

苏州街，位于后湖中心，始建于乾隆年间，又称买卖街。苏州街仿照江南水乡景色而建，建筑形式为一水两街，全长约300米，设有64处各式店铺，14座牌坊和8座小桥，是供清代居住在园内的皇后和妃子们游玩散心的集市。

The Suzhou Street, also known as the Buy and Sell Street, is located at the center of Rear Lake. It was a shopping street built during Qianlong's reign according to a typical street scene in the lower Yangtze valley. In the Qing Dynasty, this 300-meter-long street was where empresses and imperial concubines took a stroll in times of leisure. Along the shores of Rear Lake are 64 shops, 14 archways and 8 bridges, including teahouse, restaurant, bank, drugstore, pawnshop, dye-house and publishing house.

1 沿水而建的苏州街
  Street along the River
2 豳风桥
  Binfeng (Customs of Bin State)Bridge
3 十七孔桥
  17-Arch Bridge

圆明园
Yuanmingyuan

　　圆明园，始建于清康熙四十八年（1709年），是清代"三山五园"之首，在鼎盛时期有"万园之园"和"东方凡尔赛宫"的美誉。

　　圆明园是圆明园、长春园和万春园的总称，占地约350万平方米，其中40%为水域，规模宏伟，景色秀丽，拥有140余处景点，是当时世界上最大的皇家园林。园内建有楼台殿阁、亭榭轩馆等各式古代建筑200余座，同葱郁连绵的山丘、回环萦绕的河湖，以及茂盛的林木和芬芳的花草，构成了一座精美绝伦的园林博物馆。

　　圆明园是集中国古代园林建筑艺术之大成的杰作，园内模仿建造了全国各地的许多风景名胜，最为著名的有仿杭州西湖十景等。与中国其他古典园林不同的是，圆明园内还建有西式园林建筑，是由郎世宁等西方传教士设计指导，中国工匠建造，具有意大利文艺复兴时期的风格，但在造园和建筑装饰方面也吸取不少中国传统手法。著名的景观有大水法、观水法、万花阵等。

　　可惜的是，这座堪称世界之冠的皇家园林，于1860年被入侵北京的英法联军疯狂劫掠后烧毁。1900年，八国联军再次洗劫了圆明园，使园内建筑和古树名木遭到彻底毁灭。闻名世界的万园之园变成一片废墟，只有通过断壁残垣可以一窥它昔日的辉煌。如今，圆明园遗址已经得到重点保护，并在原处建立了遗址公园。

The Yuanmingyuan (Garden of Perfection and Brightness), first built in 1709, the 48th year of the reign of Emperor Kangxi, was one of the five most famous gardens built during the Qing Dynasty. It was extolled as the "Garden of All Gardens" and "Versailles of the Orient" in its heydays.

Yuanmingyuan had an area of 350 hectares, 40 per cent of which was covered by water, and it was a collective name of Yuanmingyuan, Changchunyuan (Garden of Eternal Spring) and Wanchunyuan (Garden of Everlasting Spring). It was a vast landscaped garden at once grand in scale and enchanting in scenery, and once boasted the largest royal garden in the world with its more than 140 scenic attractions. In Yuanmingyuan, there were also some two hundred buildings — halls, towers, terraces, pavilions, corridors, pagodas, bridges — of different sizes and styles. All these, the green

大水法建筑群遗址
Relics of Dashuifa Complex

hills, exquisite architectures, and limpid waters, were laid out with picturesque appeal, and decorated with thriving trees and beautiful flowers, making Yuanmingyuan a landscaping and horticultural miracle.

The construction of Yuanmingyuan embodied the fine traditions of Chinese gardening and the refined skills of Chinese art and architecture. And, what more, many of the China's famous scenic spots were imitated in the garden. Most famous of these, for instance, were the ten most beautiful sights at the West Lake in Hangzhou, Zhejiang Province. Yuanmingyuan differed from other classical gardens in China in that its typical Chinese scenery was mingled with Western architecture. The complex of

Western-style buildings were designed by Western missionaries such as Girseppe Castiglione, and constructed by Chinese artisans. Built mainly of finely engraved stone and in the style of the Renaissance, however, the buildings were decorated with glazed-tiled roofs, a typical Chinese architectural method. Such buildings include Dashuifa (Grand Waterworks), Guanshuifa (Throne for Viewing the Waterworks), and Wanhuazhen (Labyrinth of Ten Thousand Flowers).

In 1860, unfortunately, Anglo-French Allied Forces, ordered by Earl of Elgin, sacked and looted Yuanmingyuan, and burned it to the ground. A world-famous garden was thus reduced to ruins. In 1900, the Eight-Power Allied Forces made further damage to

this garden. The invaders took away everything valuable. Its former beauty and glory no more, the entire garden lay in clusters of ruins and debris. Only does the stone and marble remains of fountains and columns hint at how fascinating the original must once have been. Today the ruins of Yuanmingyuan have been put under key protection by both the district and municipal governments. A park was established at the site, and some of the original structures and scenic spots have been restored.

1.2.4 大水法建筑群遗址
Relics of Dashuifa Cornplex
3 鸟瞰圆明园
A Bird's-Eye View of Yuanminyuan

北京是中华民族文化的摇篮，也是人类文明的发祥地之一，早在50多万年前，就有人类在此生息、繁衍。北京，地理位置优越，地处连接东北与中原、西北的咽喉之地，历代统治者对北京的建设，都予以了高度的重视。因而即使是在没有成为国都的年代中，北京也以全国北方政治、经济、军事、文化中心的地位巍然耸立。在成为国都的800余年中，各朝各代对北京的建设、巩固与发展更是尽其所能、不遗余力。经过漫长的积累，北京形成了布局宏阔、宫殿辉煌、府第精美、文化灿烂、宗教相融、商贾云集的"世界之都"。

悠久的历史为北京留下了无数具有极高审美价值和文化价值的胜迹。北京现有文物3550处，其中，全国重点文物保护单位60处，市级文物保护单位234处。此外，北京已拥有联合国教科文组织批准的6项世界遗产项目。这些珍贵的历史文物就像颗颗璀璨的珍珠，在北京的大地上熠熠生辉。

文物古迹

Places of Historical Interest

Reputed as a "cradle of the Chinese Civilization" and "Birthplace of the Culture of Mankind", Beijing's long and illustrious history started approximately some 500,000 years ago. It is here that the ancestors of modern Homo sapiens, Peking Men, lived in caves, which, in some sense, was their choice by nature. The development and prosperity in the later generations are the inevitable results of history. Geographically, Beijing is a gateway to Northeast, Northwest China and the Central Plain, and that's why rulers of all past dynasties attached great importance to the construction of Beijing, even though it didn't serve as the capital but as the center for politics, economy, military affairs, and culture in North China, hence making it the Capital of the World with grandeur layout, magnificent palaces, elegant mansions, brilliant culture, harmonious religions, and bustling commerce.

A long history has left numerous famous historical sites which possess great aesthetic and cultural values. Currently it boasts 3,550 monuments and cultural relics, among which 60 are under state protection, 234 are under municipal protection, and 6 are inscribed on the List of World Heritage by the UNESCO. These relics of historic value are like pearls shining on the land of Beijing.

长城
Great Wall

　　万里长城，东起辽宁鸭绿江畔，西至甘肃嘉峪关，横跨几个省、自治区、直辖市，绵延7350千米，像一条巨龙奔腾在中国辽阔的北方。它是中国古代劳动人民智慧与血汗的结晶，是中国古代文化的象征和中华民族的骄傲。

　　长城，是中国古代一项伟大的军事防御工事，被誉为"世界七大建筑奇迹"之一。其建造始于公元前7世纪的春秋战国时期。各诸侯国为了抵御别国的侵略，各自修筑城墙、驻兵防守。公元前221年，秦始皇统一中国，为了防范北方游牧民族的侵扰，将原来秦、燕、赵等诸侯国的城墙连接起来，经过重修、加固、增筑，形成了中国历史上第一道"万里长城"。此后历朝各代皆有增建，至今保存仍然完好的长城大多数是明朝修筑的。长城大都筑于崇山峻岭之上，墙体随山势而建，非常壮观。在设计和施工上，体现了当时军事家和施工者的聪明才智，他们用"因地形、用险制塞"和"因地制宜，就地取材"的方法，解决了防御的需要和在不同地区、不同条件下筑城的难题。在长城上还建有规模、等级不同的城堡、墩台、关口、烽火台等。

　　北京地区的长城是万里长城中最富特色、保存最完整的一段，也是明代长城的精华部分。1567年，明王朝著名将领戚继光任蓟镇总兵，亲自督修辖区内的长城。十几年间，东起山海关，西止居庸关，城墙高峙，墩台林立，烽火相望，成为保卫京师的坚固防线。长城在北京地区内长约629千米，从平谷将军关入境后，经怀柔、密云、昌平、延庆、门头沟六个区县，其建筑修建遵循"因险制塞"的原则，呈半环状蜿蜒起伏于崇山峻岭间。其中，八达岭、居庸关、慕田峪、司马台、古北口、沿河城等雄、险、秀、奇，各具特色，令人叹为观止。

　　长城是世界建筑史上最伟大的工程之一，它留给后人的历史、文化、艺术、建筑等珍贵的价值，都将永存人间。1987年，联合国教科文组织将长城作为文化遗产项目列入《世界遗产名录》。

　　Known in China as the Ten-Thousand-Li Long Wall, the Great Wall stretches for 7,350 kilometers from the banks of the Yalu River in Liaoning Province at the east end to Jiayuguan Pass in Gansu Province at the west end. Rising and falling, twisting and turning like a dragon on the vast tract of land in North China, it is the essence of wisdom and hard toil of the ancient Chinese people, as well as a symbol of ancient Chinese

长城雪景

Snowy Scene of the Great Wall

文物古迹·长城

culture and the pride of the Chinese nation.

Originated as a military bulwark in ancient times, the Great Wall is one of the seven construction wonders in the world. Its Construction started in the 7th century B.C. The vassal states under the Zhou Dynasty each built their own walls for defense purposes. In 221 B.C. when Emperor Qin Shi Huang conquered all the other six vassal states and became the first emperor of a unified China, he ordered to link these walls up and rebuild, reinforce, and extend them, which finally shaped the original Great Wall in Chinese history. Reinforcement of the Great Wall continued throughout the following dynasties for more than two thousand years. The present Great Wall is mainly remains from the Ming Dynasty. The majority of the Great Wall is built along the ridges of the mountain chains, and kept changing in height and width, looked imposing and magnificent. Construction was carried out in line with local conditions and by drawing on local resources. Serving as an impregnable military defense, this great work was comprised of architectures of different grades, forms and uses, such as castles, block-houses, fortresses, passes, watchtowers, beacon towers, and additional wall structures.

The section of the Great Wall in Beijing area is known as the most distinctive and best preserved. In 1567 during the Ming Dynasty, the famous general Qi Jiguang was appointed as frontier officer of the Ji Town. He personally supervised the reconstruction of the Great Wall within his territory. Starting at the Shanhaiguan (Mountain and Sea) Pass in the east and terminating at the Juyongguan Pass in the west, the wall was standing with numerous watchtowers and connected by countless beacon towers. It became a rugged line of defense guarding the capital. The Great Wall enters Beijing area at the Jiangjunguan (General) Pass in Pinggu District, and stretches across totally six districts or counties including Huairou, Miyun, Changping, Yanqing, and Mentougou, lengthening 629 kilometers. With passes built on sheer cliffs and strategically passes, the wall climbs up and down, turns and twists on the high mountain ridges in Beijing area. Of the wall, the sections of Badaling, Juyongguan Pass, Mutianyu, Simatai, Gubeikou, Yanhecheng are distinctively featured by grandness, steepness, beautifulness, and oddness and acclaimed as the acme of perfection.

The Great Wall, one of the greatest projects in the world architecture, stands as a precious witness to history, and its value in culture, art, and architecture seems to be immortal. In 1987, the United Nations Educational, Scientific and Cultural Organization (UNESCO) inscribed the Great Wall on the World Heritage List.

1 长城腾挪跌宕，气势磅礴
The Great Wall runs up and down the mountains with a tremendous momentum.

文物古迹·长城

95

八达岭长城，位于延庆县军都山的崇山峻岭之上，始建于明弘治十八年（1505年），是居庸关的外口；因在居庸关之北（位于关沟北口），也叫北口，为居庸关的重要前哨，也是明代首都北京的重要屏障。八达岭居高临下，地势非常险峻，自古便有"居庸关之险不在关，而在八达岭"的说法。八达岭关城，东西各建关门一座，东关门刻有额题"居庸外镇"，西关门额题为"北门锁钥"，都是砖石结构，券洞上为平台，南北两面各开一豁口，接连关城城墙。台上四周有砖砌垛口。一条大道连接两门，地势非常险要。

登上八达岭长城远眺，长城蜿蜒在崇山峻岭之上，如巨龙奔腾，景象壮观。城墙平均高7.8米。墙基用巨大花岗岩条石砌成，墙身高大坚固，墙顶可容5马并进、10人并行。城墙外侧建有垛口，供巡逻、瞭望之用，射击孔可以射箭。每隔500米左右设有敌楼、墙台，用于住宿、存放兵器和放哨守城。

八达岭长城，山势险峻、风光无限，是万里长城向游客开放最早的地段，知名度也最高。该景区的独特之处在于其历史文化和大自然的互相融合。这里四季分明，春如花海，夏拂清风，秋似丹染，冬披银装，一派塞外风光。

The Great Wall at Badaling, built in 1505, or the 18th year of Ming Emperor Hongzhi's reign, is located on the ridges of Jundu Mountain in Yanqing County. A defensive outpost of the Great Wall, Badaling is at the highest point of north end of the Guan'gou gorge, in which the Juyongguan Pass lies. In the history, it guarded the north entrance of Juyongguan Pass and served as a gateway to Beijing, the capital. Looking down from the height, Badaling is strategically located and difficult of access, hence the saying, "The most difficult part is not at Juyongguan Pass but at Badaling." The Badaling fortress is flanked by two stone-and-brick-built gate towers, which is linked with a road. The tablet inscribed with "the Outpost to Juyongguan Pass" is hung on the eastern gate and another

文物古迹·长城

1　八达岭长城
　　Great Wall at Badaling
2　八达岭长城秋色
　　Badaling in Autumn
3　完善的防御体系
　　Complete Defense System

arrows. Watchtowers and battlements are built at 500-meter intervals, where soldiers took up their lodgings, stored their weapons and keep guard.

Badaling is the earliest section of the Great Wall to be opened for visitors with dangerous mountain slopes and splendid scenery, and the most famous section. The climate at Badaling is marked by four distinct seasons. In spring the place is taken over by a riot of flowers; in summer the wind blow gentle and soothing; in autumn the mountains are dyed crimson by autumn leaves; and in winter the entire place puts on a thick snow mantle.

1 巨龙游弋
  A Giant Dragon
2 历史的见证
  Ancient Wall in Witness of History
3 八达岭长城雄姿
  Great Wall in Majestic Appearance
4 巍然屹立
  Imposing Towers

one "the Lock on the Northern Gateway" on the western gate. On the gate arches are platforms, which are crenellated with merlons.

The top of Badaling provides a general view of the surroundings. Watchtowers and battlements are seen on the mountains south and north. The Great Wall threads its way through a jumble of mountains like a giant dragon. The wall here is tall and sturdy, at an average height of 7.8 meters, and stands on a base built of huge granite slabs. The top of the wall is wide enough for five horses or ten men walking abreast. Crenellations are built atop the outer wall for observational purposes, and there are also embrasures to facilitate the shooting of

3

4

文物古迹·长城

居庸关，位于北京昌平区境内，这里山峦起伏叠嶂，山林枝繁叶茂，景色优美，"居庸叠翠"被誉为燕京八景之一。

居庸关处于两山夹峙的关沟之中，"一夫当关，万夫莫开"，是绝险的关隘，自古就是北京的门户。该关曾多次重建，现存关城为明代所建，总面积33500平方米。明代曾在此设"卫"，常驻守军。关城设南北门，南门筑有瓮城。关城内，还有一座非常精美的汉白玉云台。云台建于元至元五年（1268年），台基上原有三座石塔，台下有券门，叫做"过街塔"，元末明初时被毁。云台面积310平方米，券门呈半六角结构，是中国现存石券建筑中所罕见的。门上正中雕有大鹏金翅鸟，两边分别雕着金刚杵、象、龙等图案。尤其珍贵的是门洞内刻有四大天王浮雕，以及六种文字（计有梵、藏、八思巴、维吾尔、汉、西夏文）的《陀罗尼经咒》和《造塔功德记》等。洞壁还雕有2000多尊佛像，是元代雕刻艺术中具有代表性的优秀作品，有

极高的文物价值。

居庸关被誉为"天下第一雄关"。在古代，这里是兵家必争之地，曾经发生过许多战争，如辽、金、元各朝覆灭前往关外撤退时均在此发生激战。1644年，李自成领导的农民起义军也是从这里破关而入，从而推翻了腐朽的明王朝。

居庸关一带，还有马神庙、角楼、吕祖庙、长短亭、牌楼、饮马泉、金柜山、弹琴峡、五郎影等景点。

Juyongguan Pass is located in Changping District. The slopes on both sides of this narrow pass are carpeted by a dense growth of foliage, which used to be one of the eight famous scenic spots in Beijing and known as Juyong Diecui (Piled Verdure at Juyong).

Serving as a gateway to Beijing, the pass is sandwiched by sheer cliffs, and the place looks so thrilling that one man alone could keep 10,000 enemy soldiers at bay. It provided impregnable protection to northwest Beijing and was one of the most important fortifications in ancient times. The Juyongguan fortress experienced several renovations in history, the present structure, covering an area of 33,500 square meters, was built during the Ming Dynasty. After its construction, a military office was set up there. The Juyongguan Pass has two gates, and a walled-in enclosure was built at the southern gate. Inside the pass is a marble platform called Yuntai (Cloud Platform) finely built in 1268, or the 5th year of the Zhiyuan Reign of the Yuan Dynasty. It

1 居庸关全景
A Panoramic View of Juyongguan

2 居庸关关城
Juyongguan Fortress

文物古迹·长城

2

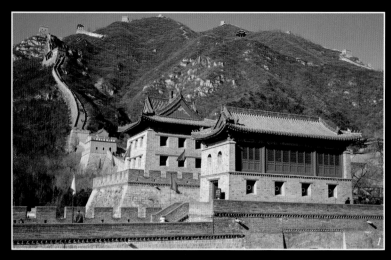

was also called Guojieta (Crossing Street Dagoba), since its half-hexagonal-arch gateway spanned the main street of the pass and there used to be three dogobas on the top of the platform, which were unfortunately des-troyed in the late Yuan and early Ming dynasties. Later a temple was built on the site, but was also destroyed. On the terrace are the remains of stone pillars and balustrade richly decorated with dragon heads, flowers and other carvings. With an area of 310 square meters, the platform is a rarity in China's stone structures. Over the gate there are carvings of a roc with golden wings accompanied by elephants and dragons. On the walls of the arch there are relief of four maharajas and inscrip-tions of religious sutras and merits and virtue for the construction of the pago-das in six languages, such as Sanskrit, Tibetan, Basiba, Uygur, Han, and Xixia. There are also more than 2,000 Buddhist statues, which are the most representa-tive masterpiece of the Yuan Dynasty. These beautiful relief works are rarely seen in China, and possess very high cultural value.

Reputed as the "Number One Impos-ing Pass under Heaven", Juyongguan Pass witnessed many important and sig-nificant battles in Chinese. Many battles took place here, such as the wars prior

the decline of the Liao, Jin, and Yuan dynasties. In 1644, the troops of Peasant Uprising led by Li Zicheng took over Beijing and entered the city from here.

Additionally, around the Juyongguan Pass are such scenic spots as Mashenmiao (Temple of the God of Horse), Corner Tower, Luzumiao (Temple of Patriarch Lu Dongbin), Changduanting (Long-and-Short Pavilion), archway, Yinmaquan (Horse-Drinking Spring), Jinguishan (Gold Cupboard Hill) and Tanqinxia (Gorge of Playing Qin).

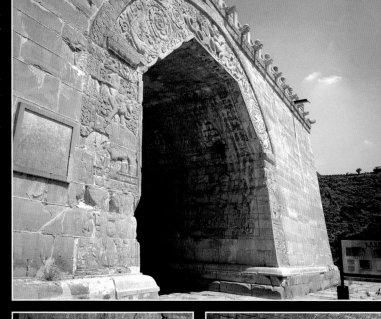

城楼前后纵置
Towers Standing One after Another

居庸叠翠
Juyong Diecui

从云台看居庸关城楼
Arch of the Cloud Platform

云台
Cloud Platform

云台内的经文
Buddhist Sutra

云台内的浮雕
Relief on the Wall of the Arch

城墙逶迤
Winding Walls

慕田峪长城位于怀柔区境内，始建于北齐年间，现存建筑为明代修建。该段长城西连居庸关，东接古北口，盘亘于险峰翠谷之中，是拱卫明京师的要塞，也是保护明帝陵的屏障。这里植被丰富，草木茂盛，果树成林，林木覆盖率达90%以上，长城如一条巨龙，游弋在绿色的海洋之中，壮观无比。

慕田峪长城大都保存完好，城墙均建在外侧山势陡峭、内侧较为平缓的地段，墙体两侧用花岗条石包砌。与其他地段长城不同处是，慕田峪长城墙顶两边都建有垛墙，防御工程极为完善。慕田峪长城敌楼密集，在2000多米的城墙上建有20多座敌楼，样式奇特，结构富于变化。

长城的正关台建于1404年，三座敌楼比肩而立，中间一座体高势伟，两侧敌楼体小室窄。三座敌楼之上均建有望亭，关门不由关台正中开设，而在关台东侧建有内外券门，由陡坡上筑成台阶，供卫戍将士上下通过。其造型独特，为长城沿线其他关口所少见。

慕田峪长城风景旅游区，山峦叠嶂，松柏苍翠，树龄百年以上的古松有200多株，"迎客松"、"鸳鸯松"、"王冠松"、"卧人松"等名木古树极富观赏价值。

Located in Huairou District, the Mutianyu section of the Great Wall was

1 **慕田峪正关台**
Mutianyu Fortress
2 **慕田峪长城**
Great Wall at Mutianyu

originally built during the Northern Qi Dynasty in the mid-sixth century, and what now remains is the main restoration made during the Ming Dynasty. Connected with Juyongguan Pass in the west and Gubeikou in the east, Mutianyu section of the Great Wall, built along steep ridges and deep valleys, used to serve as the northern barrier defending the capital and the imperial tombs during the Ming Dynasty. The surrounding natural environment of Mutianyu is most attractive. Here the mountains are densely covered by verdant plants and trees. With vegetation, green pines and cypresses covering 90 per cent of the area, the scenery here are beautiful all the year round. The dragon-like Great Wall winding in this green ocean, offers a spectacular scene.

Mutianyu, built mainly with granite, is mostly in good condition at present. Stretching along the rising and falling ridges, it is one of the most dangerous parts of the Great Wall. Outside the wall the mountains are steep while within the

3 慕田峪长城牛犄角边
   Bull's Horn Ridge of Mutianyu
4 慕田峪长城
   Great Wall at Mutianyu
5 地势险峻
   Great Wall Standing on the Ridges

文物古迹·长城

wall the land is gentle. Most parts of the Great Wall have outer defensive parapets to provide cover for the soldiers and a low parapet on the inner side to prevent soldiers or horses from falling. However, in this section, both the outer and inner parapets are crenellated with merlons, so that shots could be fired at the enemy on both sides which forming a complete defense work. In addition, more than 20 watchtowers of various appearances have been built along its 2,000-odd-meter span, indicating its military and strategic importance.

Built in 1404, the Mutianyu Pass consists of three terraced watchtowers, one bigger in the center and two smaller on both sides. The three watchtowers are connected each inside and compose a rarely seen structure amongst all sections of the Great Wall. A gate was opened into the southern side of the platform to provide entrance to south of the Great Wall.

1 依山入云
  Great Wall Soaring into Sea of Clouds
2 冰雕玉琢
  Great Wall looks as if carved of jade
3 箭扣长城雪景
  Jiaokou Great Wall after Snow

以"惊、险、奇"著称的司马台长城，位于北京密云县东北的古北口镇境内，是中国保留明代原貌的古建筑遗址之一。古北口长城，是华北平原通往内蒙古草原的要道，与居庸关东西对峙，是明朝首都的重要门户，自古即称为雄关，因此建筑特别坚固；而司马台长城，是扼守古北口长城东部的重要关口。

司马台长城，始建于北齐年间，明代重修。这段长城修建在燕山峰巅之上，绵延19千米，地势险峻，工程浩繁，敌楼众多，建筑奇特，造型多样。城墙有单面墙、双面墙、梯形石墙、垛口障碍墙等；敌楼有两层、三层、扁形、圆形；顶部有平顶、船篷顶、穹隆顶，有"长城建筑之最"的美誉。

司马台长城，以峡谷分为东西两段，一座跨谷索桥横贯其间。最高处为"望京楼"，晴天登楼远眺，叠翠美景尽收眼底，并可望及北京城，因此而得名。望京楼，屹立在海拔近千米的山巅，需登"天梯"而上。天梯高达百余米，坡度85度，几近垂直，砖石砌就的台阶仅可容脚，两侧悬崖陡壁，无胆量者绝难征服。另一座"仙女楼"，以建筑精巧著称。位于司马台北山的单边墙长城，是最为险峻的一段。这里山脊单薄，为防御需要，在仅有两块砖厚度的山脊上垒成长墙，有的地方仅有40厘米宽，其下即为悬崖绝壁，建筑非常有难度。司马台长城被长城研究专家罗哲文教授誉称为："长城是中国的建筑之最，而司马台长城是中国的长城之最。"

4

Known for dangerous and grotesque terrains, Simatai is located in Gubeikou Town in the northeast of Miyun County. It is one of China's existing ruins of ancient structure with the original look of the Ming Dynasty. The Great Wall at Gubeikou was a gateway between North China Plain and Inner Mongolia. It faces Juyongguan Pass and played a special part in the Ming Dynasty, known as the Impregnable Pass for its solid structure. Simatai is an important pass at the eastern end of the Great Wall at Gubeikou.

Hanging precariously onto the Yanshan Mountain, Simatai Great Wall was first built in the Northern Qi Dynasty

1 司马台长城望京楼
  Wangjinglou
2 司马台单边墙长城
  One-Side-Wall
3 司马台长城
  Great Wall at Simatai
4 俯瞰司马台长城
  A Bird's Eye View of the Great Wall at Simatai

and rebuilt during the Ming Dynasty. Ingeniously conceived and uniquely designed, Simatai has different characteristics. Compared with other sections of Great Wall, Simatai is densely dotted with beacon towers. Its structure is unique in that it contains single and double walls and assumes a trapezoidal shape. The watchtowers are round or ablate in shape and composed of two or three floors. Even the roofs of the tower are also diverse: some are flat, some look like the awning of a boat, and some are domical shapes. All these have earned it the reputation of being the most beautiful section of the Great Wall.

Simatai Great Wall is separated into two parts by a valley, namely the east part and west part. The highest part of the Wall is called Wangjinglou (Watching Beijing Tower). Looking into the distance in bright days, one can get a panoramic view of the rolling mountains and ranges, and Beijing proper, hence its name. The tower stands on the summit of a mountain nearly 1,000 meters above sea level. The brick-and-stone steps leads as high as 100 meters up to the tower, in 85 degrees. Don't try to climb if you are not bold enough because both sides of the stairway are sheer cliffs. Another famous building is the Fairy Tower which is the most beautiful of all towers and known for its exquisite architecture. On the northern side of the Simatai Mountain, the ridges are very narrow, some sections being only 40 centimeters. Down below are dangerous precipices, which added difficulty to the construction of the wall. To strengthen defense capabilities, a wall as thick as two bricks was built to connect the watchtowers. Therefore, it is called "One-Side-Wall". No matter the famous specialist of Great Wall, Professor Luo Zhewen, said: "The Great Wall is the best of the Chinese buildings, and Simatai is the best of the Great Wall."

1 司马台单边城长城
  One-Side-Wall
2 铜墙铁壁
  Impregnable Bastion of Iron
3 危岭绝壁
  Wall on the Edge of Vertial Cliff
4 长城雪景
  Snowy Scene of the Ancient Great Wall

3

4

文物古迹·长城

1

2

3

1 古北口长城
  Great Wall at Gubeikou
2 沿河城长城
  Great Wall of Yanhecheng
3 沿河城长城
  Great Wall of Yanhecheng

明十三陵
Ming Tombs

　　明十三陵位于昌平区，是明朝迁都北京后13位皇帝的陵墓群，并葬有皇后23人和贵妃1人，以及数十名殉葬宫人。它是中国现存规模最大、帝后陵寝最多的皇陵建筑群之一。

　　明十三陵于1409年开始营建，至1644年明朝灭亡，工程前后历经200余年。长陵是明成祖朱棣的陵墓，也是明十三陵中营建最早的陵墓。其他12座帝陵分别坐落在长陵两侧，按时间顺序依次为献陵（仁宗朱高炽陵）、景陵（宣宗朱瞻基陵）、裕陵（英宗朱祁镇陵）、茂陵（宪宗朱见深陵）、泰陵（孝宗朱祐樘陵）、康陵（武宗朱厚照陵）、永陵（世宗朱厚熜陵）、昭陵（穆宗朱载垕陵）、定陵（神宗朱翊钧陵）、庆陵（光宗朱常洛陵）、德陵（熹宗朱由校陵）、和思陵（思宗朱由检陵）。

　　陵区三面环山，中间是约40平方千米的小盆地，南接北京平原，形成陵区的天然门户；入口左右有两座山——蟒山和虎峪，像一对把门的武士守卫着陵区。十三座陵墓分布在东、北、西三面。各陵各以一座山峰为背景，规模大小不一，形制却基本相同，依次为石桥、陵门、祾恩殿、棂星门、石五供、明楼和宝城。陵区既是一个整体，各陵又自成格局、特色各异。松柏青翠，杨柳依依，衬托着红墙金顶的明楼和殿阁，构成了一幅绚丽多彩的画卷。

　　当年封建皇帝的禁园，而今成了游览胜地。1961年，国务院公布明十三陵为第一批全国重点文物保护单位。2003年7月召开的第27届世界遗产大会上，联合国教科文组织世界遗产委员会将明十三陵和南京明孝陵列入《世界遗产名录》，作为文化遗产项目"明、清皇家陵寝"的附属项目。目前向游客开放的有神路、长陵、定陵和昭陵。

　　In Changping District, northwest of Beijing, lies the Ming Tombs (or Shisanling, literally, Thirteen Tombs) — the general name given to the mausoleums of thirteen emperors of the Ming Dynasty. Besides, there entombed twenty-three empresses, one highest-ranking imperial concubine and tens of palace maids who were buried alive with their deceased masters. The Ming Tombs is one of China's largest royal mausoleums.

　　The construction of this imperial cemetery started in 1409 and took more than 200 years to complete until the doom of the dynasty. Changling, the tomb of Emperor Chengzu Zhu Di, was the earliest of the tombs, and the succeeding twelve emperors had their tombs

文物古迹·明十三陵

built around it. The other twelve tombs, in the chronologic order, are Xianling (mausoleum of Renzong Zhu Gaochi), Jingling (mausoleum of Xuanzong Zhu Zhanji), Yuling (mausoleum of Yingzong Zhu Qizhen), Maoling (mausoleum of Xianzong Zhu Jianshen), Tailing (mausoleum of Xiaozong Zhu Youcheng), Kangling (mausoleum of Wuzong Zhu Houzhao), Yongling (mausoleum of Shizong Zhu Houcong), Zhaoling (mausoleum of Muzong Zhu Zaihou), Dingling (mausoleum of Shenzong Zhu Yijun), Qingling (mausoleum of Guangzong Zhu Changluo), Deling (mausoleum of Xizong Zhu Youxiao) and Siling (mausoleum of Sizong Zhu Youjian) respectively.

The tombs are scattered over a basin approximately 40 square kilometers in area, screened by a chain of mountains on three sides and open to the Beijing Plain in the south. The burial ground at its entrance has the Mangshan Hill (Snake Hill) on the left and the Huyu Hill (Tiger Hill) on the right, symbolizing the Tombs' Entrance Gate was guarded by the "Green Dragon" and the "White Tiger". The layout and arrangement of all thirteen mausoleums are very

similar but vary in size as well as in the complexity of their structures. Each tomb complex, being against a hill, starts with a stone bridge, followed by a front gate, a stele pavilion, Ling'enmen (Gate of Eminent Favor), Ling'endian (Hall of Eminent Favor), Lingxing (Star in Charge of Study) Gates, Five Stone Sacrificial Utensils, Soul Tower and then the Precious Citadel. They show a harmonious unity but distinguished by different characteristics. Surrounded by evergreen pines and cypress trees, the entire tomb area is a unity of classic elegance of integrated natural scenery and splendor of imperial buildings.

The former forbidden ground is opened to the public. In 1961,

the Ming Tombs was inscribed on the first list of historical and cultural relic under top state protection by the State Council. In July 2003, the UNESCO World Heritage Committee at its 27th session officially inscribed the Ming Tombs and Xiaoling Tomb in Nanjing on the World Heritage List as assemblage of the Imperial Tombs of the Ming and Qing Dynasties. The Sacred Way Changling, Dingling, and Zhaoling have been opened as tourist attractions.

1 大宫门
  Dagongmen (Great Palace Gate)
2 神路
  Sacred Way

明十三陵各陵前均铺设有一条神路。其中，长陵的神路最长，计达7千米，各陵神路均由此分出，因此又称总神路。这条神路的墓仪设施种类和数量也最多，显示出兴建最早的长陵尊崇地位和宏大气势。主要建筑依次为石牌坊、大宫门、神功圣德碑亭、望柱、石像生、棂星门等。

神功圣德碑亭北面至棂星门的神路两旁，整齐地排列一组雕刻群，起首的是两座石望柱，其后为石兽、石人。共有石兽24座，依次为狮子、獬豸、骆驼、象、麒麟、马，各二坐二立；石人12座，有勋臣、文臣、武臣三种，都是立像。这组石像均用整块巨石琢成，时至今日，仍雄壮生动，基本完好，是一组很有价值的石雕艺术品。

Each mausoleum of the Ming Tombs as a Sacred Way with monumental tatuaries at the mausoleum's front. Among them, the Sacred Way of Changing, with the most diverse monumental tatuaries, is the earliest and longest. The Sacred Ways of other mausoleums all branched off from it, so it was also known as the General Sacred Way. The seven-kilometer long way starting from a stone memorial arch, leads to the front gate of Changling. Coffins of emperors were car-

tied to their final resting place in their tomb through this avenue. Along the Sacred Way orderly line the Stone Memorial Arch, Dagongmen (Great Palace Gate), Pavilion of Divine Merit Stele, Wangzhu (Watch Pole), stone statues and Lingxing Gate, which add solemn atmosphere to the cemetery.

North of the Pavilion of Divine Merit Stele is the famous avenue of stone animals and statues. It starts with two hexagonal columns, called Wangzhu in Chinese, one on each side. The animals are lions, *xiezhi*, camels, elephants, *kylin* and horses, one kneeling and the other standing, 12 on each side and 24 in total. Beyond the animals are 12 stone carvings of 4 military officers, 4 civil officials and 4 ministers of merit, 6 on each side and 12 in all, representing all officials in different ranks. As vivid as ever, these statues, each carved out of on single block of stones, are valuable stone sculptures.

3 武臣
Military Officer

4 麒麟
Kylin

长陵为明成祖朱棣与皇后徐氏的合葬陵寝，是明十三陵中规模最大、建筑保存最完整的陵墓。主要建筑祾恩殿是祭祀时行祭典礼的场所，重檐庑殿顶，面积1956平方米，建筑在汉白玉雕刻成的三层台基上，为中国最大的木结构古建筑之一。该殿是十三陵中惟一保存完好的祾恩殿，于1427年仿明朝皇宫金銮殿所建，殿顶由黄色琉璃瓦覆盖，远望金碧辉煌。大殿构件全部是楠木，不加修饰，共有60根立柱支撑着殿顶，直径最粗的达1.124米。此殿与北京故宫的太和殿、山东曲阜孔庙的大成殿并称"中国三大殿"。

Changling, the mausoleum of Emperor Zhudi and his wife Empress Xu, is the first, largest, and most complete one in all of the 13 tombs. The main structure is the Ling'endian (Hall of Eminent Favor),

5 长陵全景
A Bird's Eye View of Changling

6 长陵祾恩殿
Ling'endian of Changling

where the sacrificial ceremonies held. Built in 1427 after the model of the royal palace of the Ming Dynasty and on a three-storied marble terrace, the hall has a double-eaved hip roof, which is covered with yellow glazed tiles. This Ling'endian, covering an area of 1,956 square meters, is one of the largest wooden structures in China, and reputed as one of the Three Great Halls, the other two being the Taihedian (Hall of Supreme Harmony) in Beijing's Forbidden City and the Dachengdian (Hall of Great Achievements) in the Confucian Temple, Shandong's Qufu. Without any decoration but fabulous craftsmanship, it is supported by 60 gigantic columns of nanmu, a kind of cedar. Each of the four thickest columns in the center is 1.124 meters in diameter.

1 长陵裬恩殿
  Ling'endian
2 裬恩殿内的朱棣像
  Emperor Zhu Di's Statue in Ling'endian
3 长陵二柱门及明楼
  Double-Pillar Gate and Soul Tower

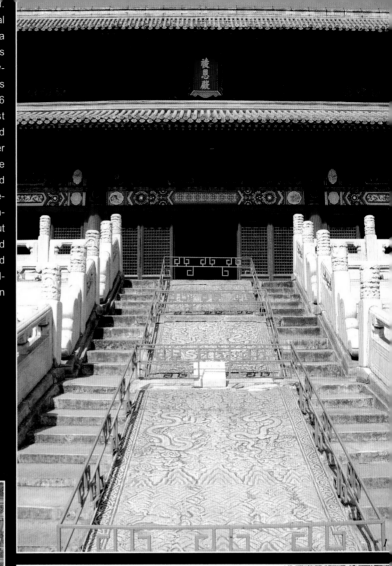

定陵是神宗皇帝朱翊钧和孝端、孝靖两个皇后的合葬墓。朱翊钧，年号万历，庙号神宗，10岁即位，在位48年，是明朝统治时间最长的皇帝。朱翊钧在他22岁时便开始动工兴建陵墓，历时6年完工，共耗白银800余万两，占地约18万平方米。定陵是十三陵中惟一一座被发掘的陵墓。地下宫殿出土各类文物共3000余件，其中以帝后生前在宫中使用的日用器物和服饰居多。

Dingling is the mausoleum of Emperor Shenzong Zhu Yijun and his two empresses, Xiaoduan and Xiaojing. Emperor Shenzong ascended the throne at the age of 10 with reign title Wanli, and ruled the country for 48 years, which made him the longest Ming ruler. The construction of his mausoleum started when Zhu Yijun was only 22 years old. It took 6 years to complete the construction. Being the most exquisite one in all 13 mausoleums, it occupies an area of 180, 000 square meters and cost more than 8 million of tales of silver. Dingling is the only one of the Ming Tombs excavated so far. More than 3,000 articles of relics and treasures were taken out from the tomb, most of which are articles for daily

定陵地下宫殿由前、中、后、左、右
5座殿堂联成，全部为拱券式石结构，总
面积1195平方米。前、中、后三殿均位于
陵区的中轴线上，其中后殿是地宫的主要
部分。后殿棺床上置放着三口棺椁，中间
是朱翊钧的灵柩，左右两边分别是孝端、
孝靖两个皇后的。两侧有26个陪葬箱子以
及散放的玉石和青花瓷瓶等。

The Underground Palace of Dingling
covering an area of 1,195 square meters
is composed of five chambers: the Fron
the Middle, the Rear Chambers, and Le
and Right Annex Chambers, among whic
the Front, the Middle and the Rear Cham
bers were designed to be on the axis. The
whole palace was made of stone. The
Rear Chamber is main part of the palace
The floor is paved with polished porphy
ritic rocks. Placed on the middle of the
stone couch is Emperor Shenzong's coffin
flanked by those of his two empresses
Around the three coffins are 26 red-lac

uered chests containing the funerary
objects, some pieces of uncut jade and
ue-and-white porcelain vases.

金刚墙
Diamond Wall

地宫中殿
Middle Chamber

3 地宫后殿
Rear Chamber

4 地宫石门
Stone Gates of the Underground Palace

5 定陵出土文物——凤冠
Phoenix Crown Unearthed from Dingling

6 定陵出土文物——金冠
Golden Crown Unearthed from Dingling

1 昭陵二柱门及明楼
  Soul Tower of Zhaoling
2 泰陵明楼
  Soul Tower of Tailing
3 裕陵
  Yuling

4 献陵
　Xianling
5 庆陵
　Qingling
6 康陵明楼
　Soul Tower of Kangling
7 思陵石五供
　Five Stone Sacrificial Utensils of Siling
8 德陵明楼
　Soul Tower of Deling

文物古迹·明十三陵

1 茂陵
  Maoling
2 永陵明楼
  Soul Tower of Yongling
3 景陵
  Jingling

周口店遗址
Zhoukoudian

周口店北京猿人遗址，位于房山区龙骨山脚下，是闻名世界的古人类遗址。1929年12月，中国考古学家裴文中先生在此发掘出第一颗完整的"北京人"头盖骨化石。它的发现奠定了直立人在人类发展中的地位，为人类起源提供了大量的、富有说服力的证据。1987年，周口店北京猿人遗址作为文化遗产项目被联合国教科文组织列入《世界遗产名录》。

"北京人"生活在距今五六十万年前，已具有与猿类不同的体质特征；拥有更大的脑量；已经学会使用原始的工具从事劳动；已懂得使用火、支配火，并学会保存火种的方法。"北京人"及其文化的发现与研究，是认识人类起源和发展的一个突破性进展。

1930年，在周口店龙骨山顶还发现约为2.7万年前的"山顶洞人"，属于人类发展晚期的智人阶段。20世纪60年代又发现了年代在"北京人"和"山顶洞人"之间的"新洞人"。2003年6月，考古人员在周口店遗址附近的田园洞发现了"山顶洞人"时期的晚期智人化石。现在，周口店遗址已成为一个向世界开放、内容丰富的人类史研究基地，在世界古人类学、考古学等领域占有重要的位置。

The Peking Man Site at Zhoukoudian, located at the foot of the Longgushan (Dragon Bone Mountain) near Zhoukoudian, Fangshan District, is the most widely known hominid locality in the world. In December 1929, Pei Wenzhong, a Chinese archae-ologist, discovered the first complete Homo erectus skull cap here, which was then named the Peking Man. The important ar-haeological discovery was earthshaking at the time and provided important material for the studies on the early biological evolution of human beings, and laid the foundation for the Homo erectus in the evolution of mankind as well. The Peking Man site at Zhoukoudian was formally inscribed on the "World Heritage List" in December 1987 by the UNESCO.

The Peking Man, who lived 500,000 to 600,000 years ago in the area, had been distinguished from anthropoid. He possessed greater capacity, and he was able to engage in creative behavior, as well as use, control and keep fire. The achievement has soon re-eived academic acknowledgement, and brought a sud-en progress in the theory of human origin and

周口店猿人洞
The cave of ape man in Zhoukoudian

1

evolution.

In 1930, the Upper Cave Man with an estimated age of 27,000 years, was discovered in the cave on top of the Longgushan. It was categorized in Homo sapiens in late development of the mankind. In 1960s, the New Cave Man, lived in the age between the Peking Man and the Upper Cave Man, was discovered. In June 2003, archaeologists found the fossils of the Homo sapiens in the late period of the Upper Cave Man in the Tianyuan Cave. Today, the Peking Man Site at Zhoukoudian has become an open research base of the history of the human being. It provides substantial contents and plays its important role in palaeoanthr-opology and archaeology.

1 第4地点洞口
  The Entrance of Loc. 4
2 猿人头像
  Head Sculpture of Peking Man
3 山顶洞人遗址
  Ruins of the Upper Cave Man
4 周口店遗址博物馆
  Museum of Peking Man Site at Zhoukou-dian

4

雍和宮
Yonghegong

雍和宫是北京市最大、保存最完整的藏传佛教格鲁派（黄教）寺院。该寺明朝时为太监的官房；清康熙三十三年（1694年），改建为清朝第三位皇帝雍正登基前的府邸。雍正三年（1725年），改为行宫、并赐名雍和宫。为团结信奉藏传佛教的蒙古和藏族人民，清王朝采取了尊奉藏传佛教的政策。乾隆九年（1744年），将雍和宫改建为藏传佛教寺庙、成为清政府管理喇嘛教事务的中心。

雍和宫规模宏伟、建筑堂皇。在整体布局上，南半部明朗开阔、清幽明静；北半部密集紧凑、格局严整。从南到北，在中轴线上排列着七进院落及殿堂，建筑形式各不相同，将汉、满、蒙古、藏等各族建筑艺术融为一体。主要建筑有天王殿、雍和宫（大雄宝殿）、永佑殿、法轮殿和万福（佛）阁等。雍和宫珍藏文物丰富多彩，堪称是中国宗教艺术的宝库。1961年，雍和宫被国务院颁布为全国重点文物保护单位。

Yonghegong (Palace of Harmony and Peace) Lamasery is the largest and most perfectly preserved lamasery of Gelug Sect (Yellow Sect of the Lamaism) in present day Beijing. It was originally used as official residence for court eunuchs during the Ming Dynasty. In 1694, the 33rd year of Qing Emperor Kangxi's reign, this building was the residence of Emperor Yongzheng when he was just a prince. In 1725 under Yongzheng's reign, it was upgraded to imperial palace for short stays away from the Forbidden City by the emperor and renamed Yonghegong. To unite the Tibetan and Mongolian ethnic groups who believed Lamaism, Qing court actively advocated and implemented the policy of respecting Lamaism. In 1744, the 9th year during his reign, Qianlong formally changed the status of the dwelling to that of a lamasery, and made it the national center of Lama administration.

Consisting of seven courtyards in a raw, the dimensions of the temple are magnificent. Generally speaking, the south structural layout in the temple is bright and spacious while the north concentrating, compact yet meticulous. Main structures including the Tianwangdian (Hall of Heavenly Kings), Yonghe-gong (Palace of Harmony and Peace, same name as the temple's), Yongyoudian (Hall of Eternal Blessing), Falundian (Hall

1 万福阁内的大佛
Giant Statue of Buddha in Wanfuge

of the Wheel of the Law) and Wanfuge (Tower of Boundless Happiness), are all aligned along the north-south central axis, with annex halls standing on both sides. The cluster of buildings in temple, including halls, pavilions and towers, is a harmonious blend of traditional Han, Tibetan, Manchu and Mongolian features. The Yonghegong Lamasery can be said a treasure house of relics. It is in deed an epitome of the religious art of China. It was listed by the State Council in 1961 as one of the historical sites under state protection.

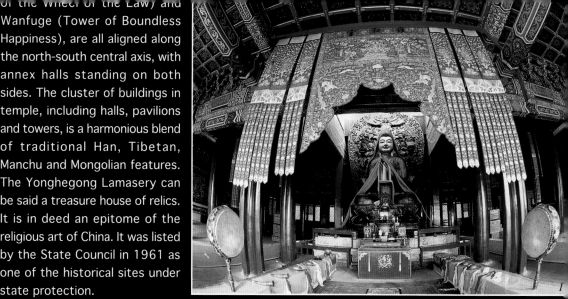

雍和宫殿前摆放有一座明代铸造的青铜须弥山，高1.5米，造型美观，雕刻精细，坐落在汉白玉雕成的椭圆形的池子里。山共分七层，顶部是小坛城，代表天堂；中间是山峦和平原，代表人类生活的地方；下部雕刻有波涛等图案。此外，山上还雕有数百颗星辰，有规律地分布在太空中，星宿之间有线相连，形成了各个星座。神奇的是，星座的分布和标记大体上符合当今天文学的研究成果。

Standing in front of the hall of Yong hegong is the Mount Sumeru, a Ming bronze sculpture. According to the Buddhist tradition, Mount Sumeru is supposed to be the centre of the world. Sitting in an oval white marble pool and 1. 5 meters in height, the Mount Sumeru consists of seven tiers. On the top of i lies the legendary paradise where Sakyamuni lives; on its middle slopes are the dwellings for mankind; and at the bottom, the floral design stands for sea waves, below which devils abide in the hell. What is surprising is that the positions of the stars and constellations roughly correspond to the findings of modern astronomy.

1 宗喀巴像
  Statue of Tsong-kha-pa

2 须弥山

万福阁，为整座寺庙中最高大宏伟的一座殿堂。阁高25米，共分三层，左右各有一座两层楼阁，东为永康阁，西为延绥阁，由飞廊相连。

万福阁内有一尊巍然耸立的大佛站象。佛像头顶接近阁顶，全身垂直高度18米，地下还埋入8米，用整根白檀木雕刻而成，雕工精细，造型宏伟，为世界最大的独木雕佛之一。

The Wanfuge, a three-storied structure, is the most magnificent building in the complex. It is 25 meters in height and flanked by the two-storied Yongkangge (Pavilion of Everlasting Health) and Yansuige (Tower of the Lasting Peace). They are connected by corridors, also known as Flying-eave, forming a cluster of majestic dignified buildings.

In the center of the Wanfuge, there is an enormous statue of Maitreya positioned on a white marble base. It is 26 meters high: 18 meters above the ground and 8 meters under the ground. The giant statue was carved exquisitely out of a single trunk of white sandal-wood, and is the largest of its kind in the world.

3 **万福阁**
  Wanfuge

4 **雍和宫全景**
  A Panoramic View of Yonghegong

北京是中华人民共和国的文化中心，既展现着中国传统文化的深邃厚重，又表现出中国当代文化的多姿多彩。

北京既有深远的风俗积淀，又融进了不同时代的特色与各国、各民族的精华，所以形成了独特的"京味儿"文化。"京味儿"文化，是以中国北方生活为基础，京城文化为内涵，汉族习惯为主体，又吸纳与融合其他文化而形成的。其体现在北京人的衣食住行、接人待物、婚丧嫁娶等各个方面。

在北京，体味这种独具特色的文化有多种方式：您可以品尝北京烤鸭和特色小吃，可以欣赏有着"东方歌剧"美誉的京剧，也可以逛逛散发着浓郁的地域特色的传统商业街。作为老百姓城市生活的依托，胡同和四合院更是北京丰富的历史文化发展演化的重要舞台，当之无愧地成为北京传统地方特色的象征。因而，到古老的胡同里漫步，参观传统的四合院是了解北京文化的最佳方式。

京城文化

Beijing's Culture

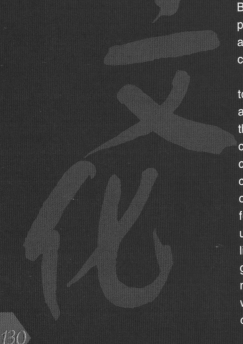

The cultural center of China, Beijing displays the pageant and profound Chinese traditional culture, as well as colorful contemporary culture of China.

Beijing has a strong flavored custom that integrates the essence of all eras and all nations. Based on the lifestyle of North China, Beijing's culture emerge with its own cultural characteristics, mostly the Han culture, while combining those of other places in China as well as foreign cultures. It contains such unique cultural phenomena as the literature, art, architecture, language, and so on, and features kind, mild, humorous and philosophical, which could be seen in all aspects: clothing, food, housing, means of traveling, communication, weddings and funerals.

In Beijing, tourists could taste Beijing roast duck and snacks of Beijing flavor; they could watch Peking Opera, which is reputed as Opera in the Orient; and they could also stroll around the traditional commercial streets. In this way, they experience the local culture. However, hutongs and quadrangles are the backing of Beijinger's lives, as well as an important stage for Beijing to showcase her long history, rich culture and development. With the strong local flavor, hutongs fully deserve the honor of being the symbol of Beijing's traditional features. Thus, to roam around hutongs perhaps is the best way to know Beijing's culture.

胡同
Hutong

　　北京的胡同可谓名扬天下，人们一提到北京的街巷，就自然而然地谈及构成街巷的胡同。胡同，是贯通城市干道的网络，是北京街巷的地方特色，北京的象征。

　　胡同，最初形成于元朝。"胡同"两字是蒙古语的译音，原意为"水井"，因为在有水井的地方居住是蒙古游牧民族的生活习惯。元大都城，始建于1267年，围绕皇城这个核心，以钟鼓楼为北边起点，直达大都城南门的城市中轴线，在全城设9条南北走向和东西走向的干道。在此基础上，随着城市建设规模的不断扩大，逐渐形成棋盘式的格局。城内，南北走向的主干道所形成的道路称为经，东西走向的主干道所形成的道路称为纬。经纬交叉划出的地界构成了坊。坊是皇城之外的居民区，坊内以东西走向为主的相距甚近的道路就是胡同。元大都城内的道路纵横交错，排列得井然有序。以后的历朝历代，都是在此基础上扩大修建的。

　　走进北京的胡同，犹如进入了博物馆，那丰厚的文化底蕴叫人叹为观止。胡同里形形色色的宅院大门，精雕细琢的砖雕，形态各异的门礅儿，参天的古木，还有影壁、石刻……无一不诉说着胡同悠久的历史，展示着古都的独特风韵。逛北京的胡同，仿佛进入了多姿多彩的画廊。胡同在那晨昏晴雨、春夏秋冬景色的变化中，展示着古都的沧桑；胡同又像一部丰富多彩的百科全书，既反映了悠远的历史，又展开了了解现代社会风情的画卷。

　　为保持北京的古都风貌，许多著名的胡同已被当作文物保留下来了。并且开展了胡同游览，展示老北京的风采。在什刹海地区，游客可以乘坐人力三轮车，结伴畅游，去看北京四合院中老百姓的日常生活，也可以登上鼓楼、俯瞰保留下来的老北京胡同格局，同时还能游览恭王府、宋庆龄故居、郭沫若故居等景点。

　　One of the unique features of Beijing is its numerous Hutongs which means small lanes. In many people's minds, Beijing is associated with the hutongs, which form the skeleton of old Beijing. Hutongs are an important part of the culture and the way of life of Beijingers, as well as the symbol of Beijing.

　　The hutong's history can be traced back to the Yuan Dynasty when the Mongols built Dadu (Great Capital), which later became Beijing. The word "hutong" is said to originate from the word "hottog" which means "well" in Mongolian. In the northern grasslands communities

tended to dig out a well and live around it. Later it was applied to small street, and the sound gradually changed to hutong. In 1267, Khublai Khan, the grandson of Genghis Khan, began to construct Dadu. He built a group

1 四通八达的胡同
  Hutong Reaching Everywhere
2 胡同游的三轮车
  Rickshaws for Hutong Tour
3 树阴下的胡同
  Hutong in Shade of Trees
4 古树映衬出胡同的沧桑
  Ancient tree, a witness of history

of structures by the waterside on the northwestern outskirts of Zhongdu of the Jin Dynasty as the center of his new capital and encircled the area with a city wall. After construction was completed, he asked all the residents who lived in the old city to move to the new one. Orderly laid out, the new capital had nine north-south streets known as *jing* (warp), and nine east-west streets known as *wei* (weft) intersecting each other and dividing the city into rectangular blocks of single-story houses grouped around courtyards, which were known as fang. The narrow roads stretching from east to west between fang are known as hutongs. The successive Ming and Qing dynasties all built their capitals on the basis of the previous dynasty.

One feels as if he entered a museum when walking along the hutongs and feeling the appeal of

1　高墙下的窄巷，反衬出胡同的幽深。
　　A narrow hutong hemmed in by high walls.
2　胡同两旁残破的墙壁讲述着它悠久的
　　历史。
　　*Dilapidated walls on both sides of a
　　hutong witness its long history*
3　胡同内的建筑，随着主人的变迁，也
　　在不断改变。
　　*With the passage of time, many hutongs
　　became narrower and narrower because
　　people often encroached on them by ex
　　panding their compounds.*
4　茂盛的树木给胡同带来一丝清凉的感觉
　　*Luxuriant trees bring hutong a sense of
　　coolness*

京城文化·胡同

the local culture, which can be seen in the front gates of compound houses, the exquisitely carved bricks, various shapes of wooden or stone blocks supporting the pivot of a door, ancient trees, screen walls facing the gate inside the courtyard, and stone carvings. Beijing's hutongs look like kaleidoscopic galleries. They seem to change with the seasons and even with the time of day; they tell the stories of old Beijing and showcase the unique flavor of the ancient capital.

Many hutongs have been reserved as relics to keep the original look of Beijing. Visitors can learn more about Beijing while looking around in the lanes, by rickshaws, in the Shichahai Lake area. People can get a panoramic view of the layout of hutongs in old Beijing on the Drum Tower, and visit the former residence of Imperial Prince Gong, the former residence of Soong ChingLing, and the former residence of Guo Moruo.

1 胡同雪景
  Hutong after Snow
2 爬山虎扮靓胡同
  Hutong Decorated by Ivy

四合院
Siheyuan

　　北京四合院，历史悠久，特色浓重，作为北京传统的住宅形式，闻名于古今中外，是中国珍贵的民族文化遗产。据史书记载，早在汉代时这一形式的民房就日臻完善，经过元、明、清各朝不断改进，四合院逐渐成为中国最具代表性的民居建筑之一。

　　这种形式的民居，有正房（北房）、倒座房（南房）、东厢房和西厢房，四座房屋在四面围合中形成一个口字形，里面是一个中心庭院，所以被称为"四合院"。四合院的建筑色彩多采用材料本身的颜色，青砖灰瓦、玉阶丹楹、墙体磨砖对缝、工艺考究，虽为泥水之作，犹如工艺佳品。

　　北京的四合院有大、中、小三种不同规格，均按古代"前堂后寝"的礼制进行布局。院子比例大小适中，正房冬暖夏凉，庭院是户外活动的场所。正房或正厅，无论在尺度上、用料上、装修的精致程度上，都优于其他房屋。长辈住正房、晚辈住厢房，妇女住内院，来客和男仆住外院，符合中国古代家庭生活中要区分尊卑、长幼、内外的礼法要求。

　　北京四合院的装修、雕饰、彩绘，处处体现着民俗民风和传统文化，表现一定历史条件下人们对幸福、美好、富裕、吉祥的追求。四合院内还种有树木、花草，环境幽雅宜人。

The quadrangles, called Siheyuan in Chinese (literally, four-side enclosed courtyards), in Beijing have a long history, and they are traditional residential compounds with houses around courtyards. According to historical records, such residences were first built during the Han Dynasty, and they were improved during the Yuan, Ming, and Qing dynasties as one of the representative residences in China.

Basically, a quadrangle consists of four houses facing south, north, east and west respectively, closed in by enclosure walls, forming the shape of Chinese character "口", hence the name. Generally speaking, the quadrangle are built with gray bricks and roofed with gray tiles. The steps are made of marble and the pillars are painted vermilion. Bricks of the wall are finely laid. They are work of art.

There are three kinds of quadrangles, large, medium, and small. All the quadrangles were built in accordance with a strict set of rules from their size and style one could tell whether they belonged to private individuals

历经沧桑的四合院
Ancient Quadrangle

1

or the powerful and rich. Well proportioned, the houses in these quadrangles are cool in the summer and warm in the winter. The courtyards are ideal for outdoor activities. The rooms facing south are better than other rooms in

1 连成一片的四合院
  Roofs Like Surging Waves
2 俯瞰四合院
  A Bird's Eye View of a Quadrangle
3 走过历史的四合院门
  Broken Wall and Ancient Gate
4 雪后的四合院
  Quadrangle after Snow

京城文化 · 四合院

terms of building material and decoration. They are usually for senior members of the family. The rooms facing east and west are for juniors. Women live in the inner courtyard, and guests and male servants live in the outer courtyard.

The fittings, decorations and paintings in the quadrangle display the local customs and traditional culture and showcase people's wish for happiness, beauty, well-being, and good luck. Beijingers like to grow trees and flowers in their courtyards, making their homes lovely and pleasant.

1 古老的四合院门
  Broken Wall and Ancient Gate
2 梅兰芳故居
  Former Residence of Mei Lanfang
3 老舍故居
  Former Residence of Lao She
4 门墩
  Decorative Stone Sculpture

京剧
Peking Opera

北京京剧，被称为中国国粹艺术，已有200多年历史。京剧因形成于北京而得名，但是它的起源还要追溯到几种古老的地方戏曲。清乾隆五十五年（1790年），四大安徽戏班进京演出，并于嘉庆、道光年间同来自湖北的汉调艺人合作，相互影响，接受了昆曲、秦腔的部分剧目、曲调和表演方法，吸收了一些民间曲调，逐渐成为一种成熟的艺术，并形成了如今相当完整的艺术风格和表演体系。京剧唱腔基本属于板腔体，以西皮、二黄为主要腔调，用京胡、二胡、月琴、三弦、笛、唢呐等管弦乐器和鼓、锣、铙、钹等打击乐器伴奏。

在表演上，根据男女性别、老少年龄、俊丑忠奸等性格特征，大致可分为生、旦、净、丑等四大行当。"生"一般是男性正面角色，"旦"多指女性角色，"净"则一般是有鲜明性格的男性，"丑"多为幽默滑稽或反面角色。在各大行当中又可分为细密的分支。用京剧脸谱上的各种颜色以象征该人物的性格、品质、角色和命运，是京剧表演艺术的一大特点，也是理解故事剧情的关键。一般来说，红脸代表忠勇，黑脸表示猛智，蓝脸和绿脸多为草莽英雄所用，黄脸和白脸含有贬义，代表凶诈之徒，金脸和银脸有神秘的含义，多是神妖。除颜色外，脸谱的勾画形式也有不同的象征意义。总的来说，颜色代表性格、不同的勾画则表示性格的程度。另外，京剧表演所穿戴的服饰也很讲究，一般分为长袍、短衣、铠甲、盔帽和辅助装饰类几种，其色彩的辉煌华丽曾使西方观众为之倾倒。

The Peking Opera has a history of 200 years and is the essence of Chinese arts, as well as an important component of Chinese culture. The Opera was so named because it was a new theatrical form evolved from several types of local operas being staged in Beijing (Peking). The origin can be traced back to several ancient local operas. In 1790 during the Qing Dynasty, four famous opera troupes from Anhui Province performed in Beijing. They costaged with artists from Hubei during the reigns of Emperors Jiaqing and Daoguang, and were influenced by other operas, such as Kunqu and Qinqiang, forming a complete style and performing system that are shown today. The musical modes in Peking Opera consist mainly of *erhuang* and *xipi*, accompanied by stringed instruments such as *jinghu* (Beijing fiddle), *erhu* (second fiddle), *yueqin* (moon-

京剧中的孙悟空
A Stage Photo of Monkey King

shaped mandolin), *sanxian* (a three-stringed plucked instru-ment), Chinese flute, and *suona* horn, in addition to drums, gongs, and cymbals.

Peking Opera roles are classi-fied according to the age and personality of the characters. There are basically four types of roles, including *sheng*, *dan*, *jing*, and *chou*. All male roles are called *sheng*, which is subdivided into *laosheng* (old man), *xiao-sheng* (yound man) and *wu-sheng* (warrior type). All female roles are known as *dan*, including *qingya* (quiet and gentle), *huadan*

1 京剧剧照
  A Stage Photo
2 花脸
  Painted-Face

(vivacious or dissolute type), *wudan* (woman with martial skills), *daomadan* (woman skilled in fighting with weapons) and *laodan* (old woman). The third role-type is known as *jing* (painted-face), portrays either people who are frank and open-minded but rough, or those who are crafty and dangerous. *Chou*, a clown, is depicted by a dab or white on the face. Peking Opera has its own set of performance, a unique artistry that combines acting, acrobatics, singing, and recitations, characterized by distinctive dancing and strong rhythms. The color scheme con-

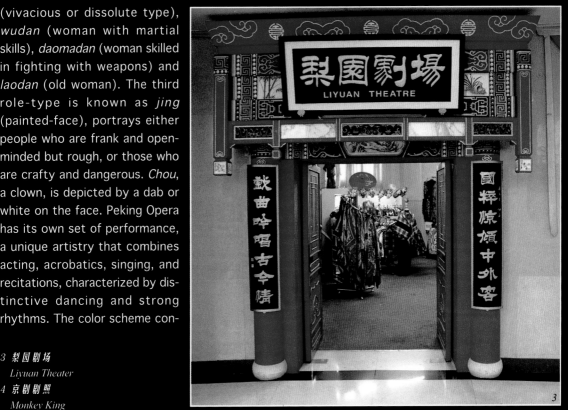

3 梨园剧场
  Liyuan Theater
4 京剧剧照
  Monkey King

京城文化 · 京剧

sists of a variety of hues on back-grounds and symbolizes the personality, role, and fate of the characters. It also serves as a key to better understand the story. Basically, red is for the loyal and bold, black for the wise and bold, blue and green for greenwood heroes, yellow and white for the savage and cruel, and gold and silver for the mysterious, mostly immortals or monsters. Additionally, the costumes are themselves objet d'art. There are generally long robes, jacket, armors, helmets and hart, and auxiliaries.

1 旦角和生角
  Dan and Sheng
2 恭王府戏台
  Theater in the Mansion of Prince Gong
3 长安大戏院
  Chang'an Theater

传统商业街
Traditional Streets

北京的传统商业街各具特色，并且都有着悠久的历史。在改革开放的今天，古老的商业街又焕发了新的活力，逐渐成为新型的商业文化区。其中最著名的有：大栅栏街、王府井大街和西单商业街。

Many traditional streets in Beijing have long history. Today, they rediate the vigor of younth with their own uniqueness. The most famous ones are the Wangfujing Street, Dazhalan Street and Xidan Commercial Street, and others.

大栅栏街，位于天安门广场西南侧，已有二三百年的历史。因百年老字号众多而享有盛名。在大栅栏不足300米的街道两旁，云集了六必居酱园、内联升鞋店、同仁堂药店、步瀛斋鞋店、瑞蚨祥绸布店、张一元茶庄、正明斋糕点铺等许多具有悠久历史的老字号。此外，全国各地的商品和旅游纪念品荟萃于此。大栅栏已经被北京市政府命名为旅游步行街。

Dazhalan Street, located southwest to the Tian'anmen Square, has long known as a commercial street in Beijing. It has a history of about 300 years. The present Dazhalan still preserves its original layout and charm. Along the less-than-300-meter street are many time-honored stores, such as the Liubiju Pickle Shop, Neiliansheng Shoes Shop, Zhengmingzhai Pastry Store, Tongrentang Medicine Store, Buyingzhai Shoes Shop, Ruifuxiang Silk and Cotton Shop, Zhangyiyuan Teahouse, and others. The street also concentrates all sorts of goods and souvenirs from around the nation. It has now been cited as a tourist pedestrian street by the municipal government of Beijing.

1 商铺云集的大栅栏
Street Lined with Time-Honored Stores
2 大栅栏街口
Dazhalan Street

王府井大街位于东长安街北侧，历史悠久，是北京最著名的商业街，被誉为"北京商业第一街"。在辽、金时代，王府井只是一个村落，元代以后，人烟逐渐稠密，当时叫丁字街。明代，这里修起了十座王府，改称十王府街。清光绪二十九年(1903年)，清政府将东安门大街两侧的商贩迁到王府井大街旁早已废弃不用的八旗兵练兵场，称为东安市场。后因这里地理位置优越，很快便成为旧京重要商业街。

新中国成立以后，北京市政府对王府井大街进行了整顿和改造，在继承和发展传统经营特色的基础上，兴建了许多大型的商业设施。800多米长的大街两侧，分布着十余个各有经营风格的大型商厦，有百货大楼、工艺美术大厦、穆斯林大厦、外文书店、新东安市场等。如今，王府井大街已经建设成为充分体现人文理念的步行街，每天来这里旅游购物的中外游人络绎不绝。

Located north to the East Chang'an Boulevard, the world famous Wangfujing Street has a long history. It is one of the most famous commercial streets in Beijing. As early as the Liao and Jin dynasties, it was a village. During the Yuan Dynasty, it was developed into a populous place named Dingzi (T-Shaped) Street. Ten mansions of princes was built along the street in the Ming Dynasty, so it was renamed Shiwangfu (Ten Mansions of Princes) Street. In 1903, the 29th year of Emperor Guangxu's reign, pedlars gathering on both sides of Dong'anmen Street were moved to the site around today's Wangfujing Street, where was a discarded drill ground for soldiers of Eight Banners, and the Dong An Plaza took shape. Then the commercial street was further developed because of its convenient location, more and more shops and foreign firms were built there, making it the most important commercial street.

Since the founding of the People's Republic, the municipal government of Beijing has renovated the street. While inheriting traditions, many large commercial establishments have been completed here, winning Wangfujing the reputation as the Number One Commercial Street in Beijing. Along the 800-meter street are 10-odd shopping malls, each with its uniqueness, including the Beijing Department Store, the Beijing Art & Craft Building, the Muslim Tower, the Beijing Foreign Language Bookstore, the Sun Dong An Market, the Oriental Plaza, and so on. It boasts an unmatched concentration of shopping malls in Beijing. A pedestrian street decorated with parterres, benches and statues has now been built here, which attracts hundreds of thousands of shoppers and visitors every day.

1 新东安市场
Sun Dong An Market
2 北京市百货大楼
Beijing Department Store

西单商业街位于天安门的西侧 2 千米，是北京最著名的传统商业街之一。其历史可以追溯到明代。当时，从西南各省进京的商旅和货物，都要经过西单进入内城各处。为此，西单这一带便有了店铺、饭馆等以招待过往旅客。明清以至到民国之时，朝廷官员、满人贵族很多都居住在西城，此后，北洋政府、国民党政府的许多机构也都设立在这里，这就进一步推动了西单商业区的发展。中华人民共和国成立后，对西单商业区进行了多次改建。如今的西单拥有著名的西单商场、西单购物中心、中友百货和个体商摊云集的西单劝业场等大型商场。除此之外，还有很多老字号和新兴商店。随着西单商业区的扩大，陆续新建或改建了西单文化广场、北京图书大厦、民航大厦，北京音乐厅、首都电影院等。古老的西单已经成为了一个富有时代特色的新型商业文化区。

Located two kilometers west to Tian'-anmen, the Xidan Commercial Street dates back to the Ming Dynasty. At the time, it was a passage for merchants and goods from provinces of southwestern China to enter the Inner City of Beijing. Then shops and restaurants were built to serve those merchants. From the Ming Dynasty to the Republic of China, many

officials and aristocrats lived in west Beijing. In addition, some departments of the Northern Warlords government and the Kuomintang government were also set up in Xidan successively, thus attributing to the commercial flourish of the area. Since the founding of the People's Republic, the government has reconstructed the Xidan commercial area many times. Nowadays, besides numerous time-honored shops, Xidan has such shopping malls as the Xidan Market, Xidan Shopping Center, and Chung Yo Department Store, as well as the Xidan

Quanye Hypermarket that gathers countless stalls. Along with the enlargement of the Xidan area, Xidan Cultural Square, Bei-jing Book Building, Civil Aviation Administration of China Tower, Beijing Concert Hall and Capital Cinema have been built here, making Xidan a new area featuring modern commercial culture.

3 *俯瞰西单文化广场*
   Xidan Cultural Square
4 *中友百货*
   Chung Yo Department Store

4

北京是著名的历史文化名城，拥有数不胜数的名胜古迹；同时，北京又是一座非常现代化的都市。新中国成立以后，特别是改革开放以来，北京发生了日新月异的变化。千年古都在新的时代又焕发出了现代化、高科技的光彩，成为最有活力和魅力的国际化大都市。申办2008年奥运会的成功，更加快了北京的发展速度。从城区到远郊，高速公路四通八达，智能化的高楼大厦拔地而起，绿地与花园成片铺开，风格特色各异的现代化标志性建筑随处可见。高楼林立的CBD、直插苍穹的中央广播电视塔、涵意深远的世纪坛、有"北京商业航母"之称的东方广场……无不具有鲜明的时代特征。

现代化的建设、古老的遗存和优美的自然环境，融合成了北京这幅以东方文化为底蕴，以现代科技为风采，以青山绿水为依托的辉煌画卷。

都市新貌

Modern Attractions

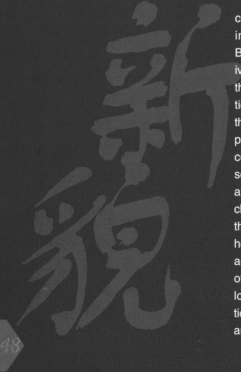

Beijing is well known as an ancient city with numerous places of historic interests. However, today's new Beijing is more charming and attractive with its growing prosperity. Since the founding of New China and particularly after the implementation of the economic reform and opening-up policies, Beijing is improving urban construction on an unprecedented scale. Its speed of development is astonishing and it brings about changes day by day, especially after the great success of Beijing's bid to host the 2008 Olympic Games. The age-old city has radiated the luster of modernization and high technology, and has become an international metropolis full of life, potential, and charm. From urban area to the suburbs, expressways reach all directions; intelligent tall buildings rise one after another; lawns and gardens are scattered here and there; and modernized symbolic structures with different characteristics can be found everywhere in Beijing. Such as, the Central Business District (CBD) of Beijing with many high buildings, the towering Central Television Tower, the China Millennium Monument having rich contents, the Dongfang (Oriental) Plaza nicknamed "Commercial Aircraft Carrier of Beijing"··· all possess the features of the times.

The ancient sites and natural environment create a harmonious Oriental culture, modern technology and natural landscape form a brilliant picture of Beijing today.

1 **长安街夜景**
 Night Scene of Chang'an Boulevard
2 **电报大楼**
 Telegraph Office
3 **中华世纪坛**
 China Millennium Monument

都 市 景 观

1 四惠立交桥
  Sihui Overpass of the Fourth Ring Road
2 金融街
  Finance Street
3 复兴门
  Fuxingmen
4 建国门立交桥
  Jianguomen Overpass

都市景观

152

1　中央广播电视塔
　　CCTV Tower
2　中国科学技术馆
　　China Science and Technology Museum
3　嘉里中心
　　Kerry Center Hotel
4　亚运村
　　Asian Games Village
5　中关村
　　Zhongguancun Street

都 市 景 观

1 东方广场
Oriental Plaza
2 东单银街
Silver Street, Dongdan
3 东二环路
Eastern Road of the Second Ring Road
4 北京西客站
West Railway Station
5 国贸中心
China World Trade Center in the Central Business District (CBD)

都
市
景
观

Sketch Map of Attractions of Beijing

北京旅游景点示意简图

圆明园
Yuanmingyuan

北海公园
Beihai Park

明十三陵
Ming Tombs
(距市区 50 千米左右
more than 50 kilometers
Beijing)

颐和园
Summer Palace

西单商业街
Xidan Commercial Street

中华世纪坛
China Millennium Monument

大栅栏街
Dazhalan Street

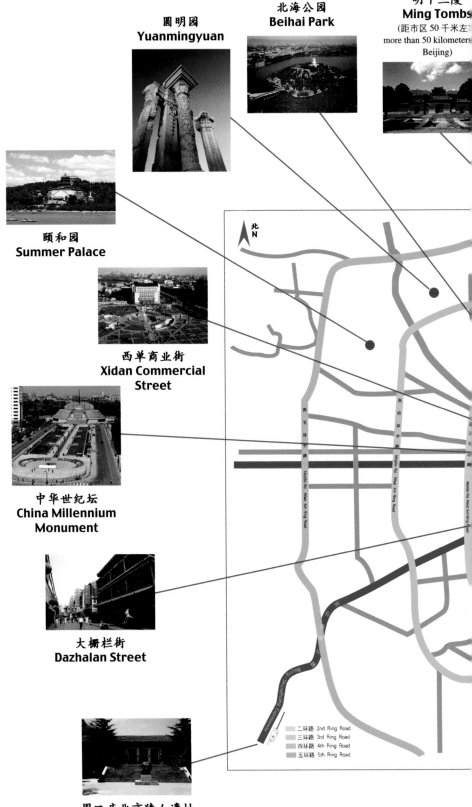

北
N

二环路 2nd Ring Road
三环路 3rd Ring Road
四环路 4th Ring Road
五环路 5th Ring Road

周口店北京猿人遗址
The Ruins of Peking Man at Zhoukoudian
(距市区 50 千米左右 　　more than 50 kilometers from Beijing)

八达岭长城
reat Wall at Badaling
(距市区 60 千米左右
re than 60 kilometers from Beijing)

居庸关长城
uyongguan Fortress
(距市区 50 千米左右
re than 50 kilometers from Beijing)

慕田峪长城
Great Wall at Mutianyu
(距市区 70 千米左右
more than 70 kilometers from Beijing)

司马台长城
Great Wall at Simatai
(距市区 120 千米左右
more than 120 kilometers from Beijing)

雍和宫
Yonghegong

故宫
Palace Museum

王府井大街
Wangfujing Street

国贸中心
China World Trade Center in the Central Business District (CBD)

天安门广场
Tian'anmen Square

天坛
Temple of Heaven

首都机场
Capital Airport

北京火车站
Beijing Railway Station

图书在版编目(CIP)数据

北京／旅舜主编.——北京：中国民族摄影艺术出版社，2005.5
ISBN 7-80069-668-5

Ⅰ．北…　　　　Ⅱ．杨…　　　　Ⅲ．城市史—北京市—画册
Ⅳ．K291-64

中国版本图书馆 CIP 数据核字(2005)第 028443 号

策　划	Planner
旅　舜	Lu Shun
主　编	Editor-in-Chief
骥　阳	Ji Yang
责任编辑	Managing Editor
鲁宝春	Lu Baochun
执行编辑	Executive Editor and Translator
王　鹏	Wang Peng
摄　影	Photographers

张肇基	杨　茵	卞志武	Zhang Zhaoji	Yang Yin	Bian Zhiwu
谭　明	谷维恒	王文波	Tan Ming	Gu Weiheng	Wang Wenbo
李　江	武冀平	吴健骅	Li Jiang	Wu Jiping	Wu Jianhua
姜景余	匡万录	王慧明	Jiang Jingyu	Kuang Wanlu	Wang Huiming
陆　岗	陆　岩	朱　力	Lu Gang	Lu Yan	Zhu Li
赵德春	王钟虎	宋　喜	Zhao Dechun	Wang Zhonghu	Song Xi

封面设计	Cover Designer
刘　佳	Liu Jia
设计制作	Art Designer
刘　彬	Liu Bin

《北京》 *Beijing*

中国民族摄影艺术出版社　出版　Publisher: China Nationality Art Photograph Publishing House

开本：787×1092mm　1/16　Format: 787 mm × 1092 mm　1/16

印张：10　Printed Sheet:10

印数：1-5000　Printed Quantity:1-5000

2005 年 6 月第一版第一次印刷　Printed Order & Impression:First Impression of First Edition in June, 200

2007 年 8 月修订版第一次印刷　First Impression of Revised Edition in August, 2007

书号：ISBN 7-80069-668-5/J.411　ISBN 7-80069-668-5 / J.411

电话：86-10-67118480　13910734033　Sales Telephone Number: 86-10-67118480　13910734033

公司网址：http://www.jdbybook.com　http://www.jdbybook.com

公司网址：http://www.旅游图书.cn　http://www.旅游图书.cn

定价：60元